THE WIV
THE PROPHET Muhammad

may the blessings and peace of Allah
be on him and his family and companions

Ahmad Thomson

Ta-Ha Publishers Ltd
1 Wynne Road
London SW9 0BB

Published by

Ta-Ha Publishers Ltd
1 Wynne Road
London SW9 0BB
www.taha.co.uk
email : sales@taha.co.uk

1st edition published in Safar 1414/July 1993
2nd edition published in 1996 and reprinted in 1998
3rd edition published in Dhu'l-Hijja 1424/January 2004

British Library Cataloguing in Publication Data
Thomson, Ahmad
The Wives of the Prophet Muhammad
1. Islam.
I. Title

ISBN 1 897940 04 1

Printed by Deluxe Printers, London NW10 7NR
Tel : 020-8965-1771
Fax : 020-8965-1772
Email : deluxeprinters1@aol.com

CONTENTS

ACKNOWLEDGEMENTS

This small book is dedicated to Shaykh Abdal-Qadir as-Sufi ad-Darqawi al-Murabit who gave me a taste of what Madina al-Munawarra must have been like in the time of the Prophet Muhammad, may the blessings and peace of Allah be on him and on his Family and on all of his Companions.

I would also like to thank Hajj Abdal-Haqq Bewley and Aisha Bewley for editing and correcting the text and for typesetting the first edition.

INTRODUCTION

What is there that a woman may not do? She can do everything except what Allah has forbidden. The teachings of Islam tell us what the limits of behaviour are. Anyone who goes beyond these limits is likely to meet trouble, both in this world and in the next world.

The best of women have lived their lives within the limits of Allah and have achieved greatness, often through actions which even the best of men could not have equalled. They have gained the love and respect not only of those who knew them, but also of those who came to hear about them long after they had died.

Among the best of women were the wives of the Prophet Muhammad, may the blessings and peace of Allah be on him and on his Family and Companions, for he ﷺ was the Best of Creation, *Al-Quthum,* the one who has all good virtues and characteristics gathered together in him, and accordingly Allah granted him the best of women in marriage.

Today, even hundreds of years later, young girls still learn a little about them and then, as they grow up and become women, they follow their example, seeking the pleasure of Allah.

This small book is for you, so that, *insh'Allah,* you will learn something that you did not know before.

It has been related by Anas ibn Malik ﷺ that the Prophet Muhammad ﷺ said, "Of all the women in all the worlds, these are enough for you [meaning that they were the best of women]: Maryam the daughter of 'Imran [and the mother of Jesus, peace be on them]; and Khadija the daughter of Khuwaylid [and the first wife of Muhammad, may the blessings and peace of Allah be on them]; and Fatima the daughter of Muhammad [and of Khadija, may Allah be pleased with them]; and Asiyya the wife of Pharaoh [who rescued Moses from the river Nile when he was a baby and brought him up as her son, peace be on them]."

Anas also related that the Messenger of Allah ﷺ said, "Love Allah for the gifts that He gives you; love me for the sake of Allah; and love the People of my House for I love them."

THE WIVES OF THE PROPHET MUHAMMAD

may the blessings and peace of Allah
be on him and his family and companions

'Abdullah ibn Ja'far reported that he heard *Sayyiduna* 'Ali ﷺ say in Kufa that the Messenger of Allah, may Allah bless him and grant him peace, said, "The best of the women of her time was Maryam, daughter of 'Imran, and the best of the women of her time was Khadija, daughter of Khuwaylid."

Is it not a great honour that the first person to embrace Islam was a woman? She was the first to bear witness that there is no god except Allah and that her husband was the Messenger of Allah ﷺ. Her husband was our beloved Prophet Muhammad, may Allah bless him and grant him peace, and she was called Khadija, may Allah be pleased with her. She was also called Tahira, meaning 'pure'.

Khadija bint Khuwaylid

Khadija, may Allah be pleased with her, came from a noble family. Her father Khuwaylid had been one of the most honoured leaders of their tribe until he was killed in battle. Her husband had also died, leaving her a very wealthy woman. When Muhammad ﷺ was still a young man, she entrusted him with some of her wealth, asking him to trade with it in Syria on her behalf. He ﷺ was already well known for his honesty, truthfulness and trustworthiness. He returned from Syria after having made a large profit for Khadija.

After hearing his account of the journey, she decided that he would make the best of husbands, even though many of the most important nobles of the Quraysh had already proposed to her and been refused, and in due course she proposed to him. After the Prophet's uncle, Abu Talib, had given the proposed marriage his blessing, Muhammad and Khadija were married. At the time of the marriage, the Prophet ﷺ was twenty-five years old, while Khadija was forty years old.

For the next fifteen years they lived happily together, and Khadija bore several children. Their first child, a son whom they named Qasim, died when he was only two years old. One more son, called Tayyib or Tahir, was also born, but he too died in his infancy. However Muhammad and Khadija also had four daughters who survived: Zaynab, Ruqayya, Umm Kulthum and Fatima.

No one – except Allah of course – knows more about a man than his wife, both his good and his bad qualities, his strengths and his weaknesses. The more Khadija came to know about her husband, the more she loved and respected him. Everyone in Makka called him '*al-Amin*', which means 'the trustworthy one', and she, more than anyone else, knew how fitting this name was.

It became Muhammad's custom each year to spend the month of Ramadan in seclusion and reflection in a cave on the mountain of Hira, which is on the outskirts of Makka. Khadija would always make sure that he was provided with food and drink during his retreat. Towards the end of one Ramadan, when he was forty and Khadija fifty-five, Muhammad suddenly appeared at their house in the middle of the night, trembling with fear and saying, "Cover me up, cover me up!"

Khadija was very alarmed to see him in such a state. Quickly she wrapped a blanket around his shoulders, and when he had calmed down, she asked him to describe exactly what had happened. He told her how a being whom he had never seen before – in fact it was the angel Jibril – had suddenly appeared to him while he was asleep and had said, "Read!"

"But I cannot read," he had replied, for he was unlettered and could neither read nor write.

"Read!" the angel had repeated, clasping Muhammad close to his chest.

"I cannot read," he had repeated.

"Read!" the angel had repeated, firmly embracing him yet again.

"What shall I read?" he had asked in desperation, and the angel had replied:

"Read, in the Name of your Lord who created,
created man from a clot,
Read, and your Lord is the Most Gracious,
Who taught with the pen,
taught man what he did not know."

(Qur'an: 96.1-5)

Although Muhammad ﷺ did not fully realise it at the time, this was the beginning of the revelation of the Qur'an; but in that first encounter with the angel Jibril, Muhammad was very frightened, for he did not know who the angel Jibril عليه السلام was or what was happening. He woke up and ran out of the cave only to find Jibril still in front of him, and whenever he turned away from him, there Jibril was in front of him yet again, filling the horizon with his mighty yet beautiful form.

"Oh Muhammad," said Jibril ﷺ eventually, "you are the Messenger of Allah and I am Jibril," and with these words he disappeared from Muhammad's sight.

After the angel had disappeared Muhammad ﷺ had clambered down the mountain as fast as he could run, not knowing if he was going mad and imagining things, or if he had been possessed by one of the *jinn*.

As she listened to Muhammad's words, Khadija ﷺ did not share any of these fears. She realised that something tremendous and awe-inspiring had happened to her husband, and she was certain, knowing him as she did, that he was neither mad nor possessed.

"Do not worry," she said, "for by Him who has dominion over Khadija's soul, I hope that you are the Prophet of this nation. Allah would never humiliate you, for you are good to your relatives, you are true to your word, you help those who are in need, you support the weak, you feed the guest and you answer the call of those who are in distress."

When Muhammad ﷺ was a little more relaxed, Khadija took him to see her cousin, Waraqa ibn Nawfal, for he was a man of knowledge, and she was sure that he would be able to explain the meaning of what had just happened to her beloved husband.

Waraqa had studied the books of both the Jews and the Christians very closely and he had learned a great deal from many of their wisest people. He knew that the coming of another Prophet had been foretold by both Moses and Jesus, peace be on them, and he knew many of the signs that would confirm the identity of this Prophet when he appeared.

After listening closely to his story, Waraqa, who was both old and blind, exclaimed, "This is the same being who brought the revelations of Allah to Moses. I wish I was young and could be alive when your people will drive you out."

"Will they drive me out?" asked Muhammad ﷺ.

"Yes," replied Waraqa. "No one has come with what you have been given without being treated with enmity; and if I were to live until the day when you are turned out, then I would support you with all my might. Let me just feel your back."

So saying, Waraqa felt between the Prophet's shoulder-blades and found what he was feeling for: a small, round, slightly raised irregularity in the skin, about the size of a pigeon's egg. This was yet another of the many signs that Waraqa already knew would indicate the identity of the next Prophet after Jesus, peace be on him.

"This is the Seal of Prophethood!" he exclaimed. "Now I am certain that you are indeed the Prophet whose coming was foretold in the Torah that was revealed to Moses and in the Injil that was revealed to Jesus, peace be on them! You are indeed the Messenger of Allah, and the being who appeared to you on the mountain was indeed the angel Jibril!"

Khadija ؓ was both overjoyed and awed to find that her understanding of what had happened on the mountain had been confirmed.

Not long after this incident, Muhammad was commanded in a subsequent revelation from Allah, through the angel Jibril, to call people to worship Allah only, and it was at this point that Khadija did not hesitate in expressing in public what she had now known for certain in secret for some time:

"I bear witness that there is no god except Allah," she said, "and I bear witness that Muhammad is the Messenger of Allah."

In the years that followed, difficult years in which the leaders of the Quraysh did everything in their power to stop the Prophet ﷺ spreading his message, Khadija ؓ was a constant source of help and comfort to Muhammad ﷺ in the difficulties which he had to face.

All her wealth was spent in the way of Allah, helping to spread the message of her husband, helping to free slaves who had embraced Islam, and helping to feed and shelter the community of Muslims that slowly but surely began to grow in numbers and strength.

The Quraysh were infuriated by the Prophet's success and did everything in their power to discourage both him and his followers, often inflicting awful tortures on them, but without success. The situation became so bad that the Prophet ﷺ told some of his followers to go to Abyssinia, where their ruler, the Negus, who was a sincere Christian, gave them shelter and protection.

Eventually there came a time when, as Waraqa had foretold, Muhammad and his followers – along with all the members of his tribe, the Banu Hashim – were driven out of the city of Makka and forced to camp out in a small ravine in the mountains nearby. This happened long after Waraqa had died, and about seven years after that extraordinary night of power in which Muhammad ﷺ had received the first revelation of Qur'an through the angel Jibril.

There, while their homes lay empty in Makka, the Muslims were exposed to the bitterly cold nights of winter and the fiery hot days of summer, with very little food and shelter. No one would buy and sell with the Muslims, or allow their sons and daughters to marry any of them. Fortunately those who secretly sympathised with the Muslims would send what food they could to them whenever the chance arose, sometimes by loading provisions onto a camel or a horse and then sending it off at a gallop in the direction of the camp, hoping that the animal would not stop or get lost before it reached its intended destination.

For three years the small Muslim community lived a life of hardship and deprivation, but although they suffered from hunger and thirst, and from exposure to heat and cold, this was a time in which the hearts of the first Muslims were both purified and also filled with the light of knowledge and wisdom. The Muslims knew that they were following the truth, and so nothing else mattered. They did not care what the Quraysh did to them or said about them. Allah and His Messenger ﷺ were enough for them!

It was during this period that the Muslims who had sought shelter in Abyssinia returned, only to find the situation even worse than when they had left it. Not long after, many of them returned to Abyssinia, their numbers swelled by those whom the Prophet ﷺ had told to accompany them.

Finally the boycott was lifted and the Muslims were allowed to re-enter the city; but the three years of hardship had taken their toll. First of all the Prophet's uncle, Abu Talib, who was by then more than eighty years old, died; and then a few months later, during the month of Ramadan, Khadija also died, at the age of sixty-five, may Allah be pleased with her.

The Prophet Muhammad, may Allah bless him and grant him peace, mourned her deeply. They had shared twenty-five years of marriage together and she had given birth to six of his children. Only one of the Prophet's future wives, Maria the Copt, would give him another child, Ibrahim, and he, like Qasim, was destined to die when he was still very young, at the age of eighteen months.

Khadija ؓ had been the first to publicly accept Muhammad ﷺ as the Messenger of Allah, and she had never stopped doing all she could to help him. Love and mercy had grown between them, increasing in quality and depth as the years passed by, and not even death could take this love away.

The Prophet Muhammad ﷺ never stopped loving Khadija, and although he married several more wives in later years and loved them all, it is clear that Khadija always had a special place in his heart. Indeed whenever 'A'isha, his third wife, heard the Prophet speak of Khadija ؓ, or saw him sending food to Khadija's old friends and relatives, she could not help feeling jealous of her, because of the love that the Prophet still had for her.

Once 'A'isha asked him if Khadija had been the only woman worthy of his love. The Prophet ﷺ replied, "She believed in me when no one else did; she accepted Islam when people rejected me; and she helped and comforted me when there was no one else to lend me a helping hand."

It has been related by Abu Hurayra ؓ that on one occasion, when Khadija was still alive, Jibril came to the Prophet ﷺ and said, "O Messenger of Allah, Khadija is just coming with a bowl of soup (or food or drink) for you. When she comes to you, give her greetings of peace from her Lord and from me, and give her the good news of a palace of jewels in the Garden, where there will be neither any noise nor any tiredness."

After the Prophet's uncle, Abu Talib, and his first wife, Khadija, had both died in the same year, the Prophet Muhammad ﷺ and his small community of believers endured a time of great hardship and persecution at the hands of the Quraysh. Indeed the Prophet ﷺ, who was now fifty years old, named this year 'the Year of Sorrow'.

In private, his dearest wife was no longer present to share his life; and in public the insults that he received from the Quraysh multiplied, now that he no longer had the protection of his dead uncle. Even when he journeyed to Ta'if, a small city up in the mountains outside Makka, to call its people to worship Allah, he was rejected and stoned by them.

It has been related by 'A'isha ؓ that on his way back to Makka, Jibril appeared to the Prophet ﷺ and said, "Allah, may He be exalted and glorified, has heard what the people have said to you and how they have responded to your invitation, and he has sent the angel in charge of the mountains so that you can tell him what you want him to do with them."

Then the angel in charge of the mountains called out to him and greeted him and said, "O Muhammad, Allah has listened to what your people have said to you. I am the angel in charge of the mountains, and your Lord has sent me so that you can order me to do whatever you want. If you wish it, I can bring the mountains on the outskirts of Makka together so that they are crushed between them."

But the Messenger of Allah ﷺ said to him, "Rather I hope that Allah will make their descendants a people who will worship Allah alone, without ascribing any partners to him."

It was a little while after this that the following *sura* was revealed:

In the Name of Allah the Merciful the Compassionate
By the morning hours
And by the night when it is stillest,
Your Lord has not forsaken you nor does he hate you,
And truly what comes after will be better for you
than what has come before,
And truly your Lord will give to you
so that you will be content.
Did he not find you an orphan and protect you?
Did he not find you wandering and guide you?
Did he not find you destitute and enrich you?
So do not oppress the orphan,
And do not drive the beggar away,
And speak about the blessings of your Lord.

(Qur'an: 93.1-11)

And so it happened.

After three years of constant struggle, a relative of his, called Khawla, went to him and pointed out that his house was sadly neglected and that his daughters needed a mother to look after them.

"But who can take the place of Khadija?" he asked.

"'A'isha, the daughter of Abu Bakr, the dearest of people to you," she answered.

Abu Bakr ☙ had been the first man to accept Islam and he was the Prophet's closest companion. Like Khadija ☙, he had done all that he could do to help the Prophet, may Allah bless him and grant him peace, and had spent all his wealth in the way of Allah. However, while the Prophet Muhammad ☙ was now fifty-three years old, 'A'isha was only a little girl of seven. She was hardly in a position to look after either the Prophet's household or his children.

"She is very young," replied the Prophet.

Khawla had a solution for everything. She suggested that he marry at the same time a lady called Sawda, the widow of Al-Sakran ibn 'Amr.

Sawda bint Zam'a

Sawda bint Zam'a, may Allah be pleased with her, had been the first woman to emigrate to Abyssinia in the way of Allah. Her husband had died and she was now living with her aged father. She was middle-aged, rather plump, with a jolly, kindly disposition, just the right person to take care of the Prophet's household and family. So Muhammad ﷺ gave permission to Khawla to speak to Abu Bakr and to Sawda on the subject.

Khawla went straight to Sawda and said, "Would you like Allah to give you great blessing, Sawda?"

Sawda asked, "And what is that, Khawla?"

She said, "The Messenger of Allah has sent me to you with a proposal of marriage!"

Sawda tried to contain herself in spite of her utter astonishment and then replied in a trembling voice, "I would like that! Go to my father and tell him that."

Khawla went to Zam'a, a gruff old man and greeted him and then said, "Muhammad son of 'Abdullah son of 'Abdu'l-Muttalib has sent me to ask for Sawda in marriage."

The old man shouted, "A noble match. What does she say?"

Khawla replied, "She would like that."

He told her to call her. When she came, he said, "Sawda, this woman claims that Muhammad son of 'Abdullah son of 'Abdu'l-Muttalib has sent to ask for you in marriage. It is a noble match. Do you want me to marry you to him?"

She accepted, feeling that it was a great honour. Sawda went to live in Muhammad's house and immediately took over the care of his daughters and household, while 'A'isha bint Abu Bakr became betrothed to him and remained in her father's house playing with her dolls.

There was great surprise in Makka that the Prophet ﷺ would choose to marry a widow who was neither young nor beautiful. The Prophet, however, remembered the trials she had undergone when she had emigrated to Abyssinia, leaving her house and property, and crossed the desert and then the sea for an unknown land out of the desire to preserve her *deen.*

During the next two years, the Quraysh increased their spiteful efforts to destroy the Prophet and his followers, in spite of the clear signs that confirmed beyond any doubt that Muhammad ﷺ was indeed the Messenger of Allah.

Perhaps the greatest of these signs during this period was the Prophet's *Mi'raj,* his journey by night on a winged mount called the *Buraq,* through the skies to the Al-Aqsa Mosque in Jerusalem where he led all the earlier Prophets who had lived before him in the prayer, followed by his ascent on the *Buraq,* accompanied by Jibril ﷺ, through the seven heavens, and then beyond the world of forms, to the Presence of Allah – where he was given the five prayers that all his true followers have done ever since.

When he described this miraculous journey to the people of Makka, they just laughed at him, even though he accurately described the Al-Aqsa Mosque to them (and they knew that he had never been there before), and even though he described the place where he had stopped for a drink on the way to Jerusalem, and even though he told them how on the way he had told a man where his lost camel was, and even though he told them that he had seen a caravan, which no one knew about, approaching Makka and that it should arrive later on that day.

Even though the Quraysh knew that the Prophet's description of the Al-Aqsa Mosque was completely accurate, and even when they eventually saw the caravan arrive, and met the man whom he had helped, and saw the place where he had stopped for a drink, they still refused to believe him.

Only *Sayyiduna* Abu Bakr, his closest companion and future father-in-law, accepted the Prophet's account of his miraculous journey immediately: "If he has said this," he said, when some scornful Makkans first gave him the news, "then it is true!"

As the enmity of the Quraysh increased, (and while 'A'isha was still a small girl), Allah prepared the way for the future growth of the Muslim community in a place called Yathrib.

During the time of the pilgrimage in Makka one year, twelve men from Yathrib, a small city two hundred miles to the north of Makka, secretly pledged allegiance to the Prophet ﷺ, swearing to worship no gods other than Allah, nor to steal, nor to tell lies, nor to commit adultery, nor to kill their children, nor to disobey the Prophet. They returned to Yathrib, accompanied by a Muslim called Mus'ab ibn 'Umayr, who taught them all that he had learned from the Prophet, may Allah bless him and grant him peace.

As a result, the numbers of Muslims in Madina began to increase, and when the time of the pilgrimage came again, this time seventy-five people from Yathrib – three of whom were women: Umm Sulaym, Nusayba bint Ka'b and Asma' bint 'Amr – pledged allegiance in Makka to the Prophet Muhammad ﷺ, this time also swearing that they would defend and protect him, even to the death if need be.

After this, the Prophet ﷺ gave his followers permission to emigrate to Yathrib, and slowly but surely, in twos and threes, the Muslims began to leave Makka. The leaders of the Quraysh realised what was happening, and decided to kill the Prophet before he had a chance to join them.

However, Allah protected the Prophet, and on the very night before the morning on which they had planned to kill him, the Prophet Muhammad ﷺ and Abu Bakr ؓ slipped out of Makka and hid in a cave called Thawr, which was to the south of Makka.

Everybody knows what happened when the people who were hunting for them came to the cave: They found a wild dove nesting in the tree that covered the mouth of the cave, across which a spider had spun its web. Anyone entering the cave would have frightened away the dove and broken the spider's web, they thought, so they did not bother to look inside it. Their pursuers were so close that if one of them had glanced down at his feet, he would have discovered them. By the decree of Allah, the Prophet Muhammad 🌟 and *Sayyiduna* Abu Bakr ⚜ were safe!

Once the Quraysh had given up the search, the Prophet Muhammad and *Sayyiduna* Abu Bakr, may the blessings and peace of Allah be on them, circled round Makka and rode northwards. Only one man, a warrior called Suraqa ibn Ju'sham, suspected their whereabouts and set off in hot pursuit, thirsting for the reward that the Quraysh had offered to anyone who captured the two men for them. As soon as he was within shouting distance of the travellers, however, his horse suddenly began to sink into the sand, and, realising that if he did not turn back, then the desert would simply swallow up both him and his steed, he gave up his pursuit, asked them to forgive him, and returned home.

After a long, hard journey the Prophet Muhammad 🌟 and *Sayyiduna* Abu Bakr ⚜ reached Yathrib amidst scenes of great rejoicing. Their time in Makka had just come to an end, and their time in Madina had just begun – for Madina is the name that was now given to Yathrib, Madina al-Munawarra, which means 'the illuminated city', the city that was illuminated by the light of the Prophet Muhammad and his Family and his Companions, may the blessings and peace of Allah be on him and on all of them.

The journey of the Prophet Muhammad and *Sayyiduna* Abu Bakr is usually called the *hijra*, and it is at this point that the dating of the Muslims begins, for it was after the *hijra* that the first community of Muslims rapidly grew, and flowered, and bore fruit.

When she was older, the Prophet ﷺ was worried that Sawda might be upset about having to compete with so many younger wives, and offered to divorce her. She said that she would give her night to 'A'isha, of whom she was very fond, because she only wanted to be his wife on the Day of Rising. She and 'A'isha always remained very close. She ﷺ lived on until the end of the time of 'Umar ibn al-Khattab.

'A'isha bint Abi Bakr

Gradually the Muslims who remained in Makka left the city and travelled to Madina to join their beloved Prophet ﷺ, and amongst them was a little girl called **'A'isha**, the daughter of Abu Bakr ؓ. Soon after arriving in Madina, 'A'isha, who was now nine years old, was married to the Prophet Muhammad ﷺ, who was now fifty-four years old. It was at this point that she ؓ left her family's household and joined that of the Prophet Muhammad.

'A'isha ؓ later reported that the Prophet Muhammad ﷺ had told her that Jibril عليه السلام came to him and showed him a picture of her on a piece of green silk and said, "She is your wife in this world and in the next world."

About her wedding, she related that shortly before she was to leave her parents' house, she slipped out into the courtyard to play with a friend: "I was playing on a see-saw and my long streaming hair became dishevelled," she said. "They came and took me from my play and made me ready."

They dressed her in a wedding-dress made from fine red-striped cloth from Bahrain and then her mother took her to the newly-built house where some women of the Ansar were waiting outside the door. They greeted her with the words, "For good and for happiness, may all be well." Then, in the presence of the smiling Prophet ﷺ a bowl of milk was brought. The Prophet drank from it himself and then offered it to 'A'isha. She shyly declined it, but when he insisted she drank as well and then offered the bowl to her sister Asma' who was sitting beside her. The others who were present also drank from it, and that was all there was to the simple and solemn occasion of their wedding.

Her marriage to the Prophet Muhammad ﷺ did not change 'A'isha's playful ways, and her young friends continued to regularly come and visit her in her own room.

"I would be playing with my dolls," she once said, "with the girls who were my friends, and the Prophet ﷺ would come in and they would slip out of the house and he would go out after them and bring them back, for he was pleased for my sake to have them there." Sometimes he would say, "Stay where you are," before they had time to leave, and would also join in their games.

"One day," 'A'isha said, "the Prophet ﷺ came in when I was playing with my dolls and he said, "A'isha, whatever game is this?'

"'It is Solomon's horses,' I replied, and he laughed."

On another occasion, during the days of the *'Id al-Adha,* two young girls were with 'A'isha in her room, singing a song about the famous battle of Bu'ath and beating a tambourine in time.

"The Messenger of Allah ﷺ came in," said 'A'isha, "and lay down with his face turned away. Then Abu Bakr came, and scolded me, saying, 'What is this musical instrument of *shaytan* doing in the house of the Messenger of Allah?' The Messenger of Allah turned towards him and said, 'Leave them alone, for these are the days of the *'Id.*'"

After a while, 'A'isha asked the girls to leave, and the Prophet ﷺ asked 'A'isha whether she would like to watch the Abyssinians who were giving a fighting display with their weapons in the mosque and she said yes.

"By Allah," said 'A'isha, "I remember the Messenger of Allah ﷺ standing at the door of my room, screening me with his cloak, so that I could see the sport of the Abyssinians as they played with their spears in the mosque of the Messenger of Allah ﷺ. He kept standing for my sake until I had had enough and then I went back in, so you can well imagine how a young girl enjoyed watching this display."

Some might have viewed the marriage of Muhammad and 'A'isha as an exceptional marriage, but then the two partners were exceptional people. The Prophet Muhammad 羇 was the last of the Prophets and the Best of Creation; and 'A'isha was a very intelligent and observant young girl with a very good memory.

'A'isha 羇 spent the next nine years of her life with the Prophet 羇, and as she grew into womanhood, she remembered all that she saw and heard with great clarity, for to be the wife of the Prophet was even more than extraordinary. So much happened around him – the Qur'an continued to be revealed, *ayat* by *ayat*, and people's hearts were constantly being turned over and transformed, including hers – and she was a witness of so much of all that took place.

It is not surprising, therefore, that a great deal of the know-ledge that we still have today, about how our beloved Prophet 羇 lived and behaved, was first remembered and then taught to others by A'i'sha 羇. It is thanks to this exceptional marriage, between a man nearing the end of his life and a woman still near the beginning of hers, that we know so much about both of them, and this is what makes it so much easier for those who wish to follow in their footsteps to try and follow their example.

Whereas Khadija 羇 was already a wise and mature woman when she married the Prophet Muhammad 羇, 'A'isha 羇 was a spirited young girl who still had a great deal to learn when she married the Prophet, may the blessings and peace of Allah be on him and them. She was very quick to learn, however, for she had a clear heart, and a quick mind and an accurate memory. She was not afraid to talk back in order to find out the truth or make it known, and whenever she beat someone else in argu-ment, the Prophet would smile and say, "She is the daughter of Abu Bakr!"

Musa ibn Talha 羇 once said, "I have not seen anyone more eloquent than 'A'isha."

'A'isha became so wise that one of her contemporaries used to say that if the knowledge of 'A'isha were placed on one side of the scales and that of all other women on the other, 'A'isha's side would outweigh the other. She used to sit with the women and pass on the knowledge that she had received from the Prophet ﷺ, and long after he had died, may Allah bless him and grant him peace, and as long as she lived, she ؓ was a source of knowledge and wisdom for both women and men.

Abu Musa once said, "Whenever a report appeared doubtful to us, the Companions of the Prophet, and we asked 'A'isha about it, we always learned something from her about it."

On one occasion, the Prophet Muhammad ﷺ said to her, "O 'A'isha, here is Jibril giving you greetings of peace."

"And on him be peace," she replied, "and the mercy of Allah."

When she was telling Abu Salama about this, she added, "He (meaning the Prophet Muhammad ﷺ) sees what I do not see."

As well as being extremely intelligent, 'A'isha became a very graceful young woman. When she first came to live in the Prophet's household as a young girl, a strong and lasting friendship grew up between her and Sawda, and Sawda took care of her along with the rest of the household.

When 'A'isha grew up, Sawda, who was by then an old woman, gave up her share of the Prophet's time in favour of 'A'isha and was content to manage his household and be *Umm al-Mumineen* – 'the Mother of the Believers' – a title of respect that was given to all of the wives of the Prophet, may Allah be pleased with them, which confirmed what the Qur'an clearly states, that no man could marry any of them after they had been married to the Prophet, may Allah bless him and grant him peace, for:

**The Prophet is closer to the believers
than their own selves,
and his wives are as their mothers.**

(Qur'an: 33.6)

And:
O you wives of the Prophet,
if any of you is openly indecent,
the punishment for her will be doubled
– and that is easy for Allah.

And whoever of you submits
to Allah and His Messenger
and has right action,
We shall give her a reward twice over
and We have prepared a generous provision for her.

O you wives of the Prophet,
you are not like any other women.
If you are fearful (of Allah)
then do not be soft in your speech,
lest someone whose heart is sick is attracted (to you),
but speak words that are wise.

And stay quietly in your houses,
and do not make a dazzling display
like that of the time of ignorance before;
and establish the prayer and pay the *zakat*
and obey Allah and His Messenger.
Surely Allah wishes to remove impurity far from you,
O People of the House,
and to purify you completely.

And remember the *ayats* of Allah
that are recited in your houses
and the wisdom.
Surely Allah is All-pervading, All-aware.

(*Qur'an*: 33.30-34)

It is sometimes difficult to picture what life must have been like for the wives and the Companions of the Prophet ﷺ because the light that emanated from him and through them was so unique. The Messenger of Allah ﷺ had no shadow – because he was light and this light illuminated the hearts and minds and understanding of his followers, giving them insight without blinding them.

The Prophet Muhammad ﷺ was truly a mercy to all the worlds, and no one with a clean heart could possibly forget this, least of all the Prophet himself ﷺ:

**O Prophet, surely We have sent you as a witness
and as a bringer of good news and a warner;**

**and one who calls (people) to Allah
by His permission,
and as a shining light.**

(Qur'an: 33.45-46)

It is said that people were awed by the Prophet Muhammad ﷺ when they were in his presence, and that they sat and listened to his words with their eyes lowered, as if they had birds perched on their heads, and that they would do anything for him, so great was their love for him.

It was because of the perfection of the Prophet Muhammad ﷺ that everyone was commanded to ask blessings on him:

**Surely Allah and His angels
pray blessings on the Prophet;
O you who believe!
Pray blessings on him
and greet him with greetings of peace.**

(Qur'an: 33.56)

It was because of the Prophet Muhammad's unique station with Allah that his wives and his Companions were expected by Allah to behave with such respect and courtesy towards the Prophet Muhammad ﷺ; and that his wives could not possibly marry anyone else after having been married to him:

When you ask his wives for something,
ask them from behind a screen.
That is purer for your hearts and for their hearts.
It is not for you to cause injury
to the Messenger of Allah,
nor ever to marry his wives after him.
To do that would be something dreadful
in the sight of Allah.

(*Qur'an*: 33.53)

During the nine years that 'A'isha ﷺ was married to the Prophet Muhammad ﷺ, she witnessed many of the great events that shaped the destiny of the first Muslim community of Madina al-Munawarra:

It was during the course of their marriage that the direction of the *qibla* was changed from Jerusalem to Makka, thereby more clearly distinguishing the Muslims from the Jews and the Christians, and it was during the course of their marriage that she must have listened to many of the Jews and the Christians and the idol-worshippers who came not to listen to the Prophet ﷺ but to argue with him, in the hope that they could find a plausible excuse to justify their rejection of him. It was through exchanges such as these that 'A'isha learned to distinguish what was true from what was false.

As the prophetic guidance continued to be revealed through the Prophet Muhammad ﷺ, 'A'isha's way of life – along with that of all the Muslims – was gradually reshaped and refined: It was during the course of their marriage that drinking alcohol was finally forbidden, that it was made clear what food was *halal* and what food was *haram*, that it became necessary for women to wear a *hijab* in public and when praying, that the guidance as to how to fast was revealed, that paying the *zakat* became obligatory on all Muslims, and that the rites of the *hajj* were purified and clarified.

In fact every aspect of life, from birth to death and everything that happens in between, was illuminated by the way in which the Prophet ﷺ behaved – and it was this way of behaviour, the *Sunna*, that 'A'isha helped to preserve and protect, not only by embodying it herself, but also by teaching it to others.

'A'isha was once asked to describe the Prophet ﷺ, and she ؓ replied that he was 'the Qur'an walking', meaning that his behaviour was the Qur'an translated into action. She did all that she could to do likewise. Thus she not only knew and embodied the *Sunna*, but also she memorised the Qur'an by heart and understood it.

It was during the course of their marriage that, amongst others, the battles of Badr, and Uhud, and al-Khandaq (The Ditch) were fought. These were the three major battles against the Quraysh, that shifted the balance of power out of the hands of the *kafirun* and into the hands of the Muslims. Although she was still very young, 'A'isha participated in them all, bringing water for the Muslim warriors, and helping to look after the wounded. She witnessed life, and she witnessed death – both in the way of Allah and in the way of the *kafirun* – and she understood both. Indeed one of the meanings of her name, 'A'isha', is 'life'.

It was during the course of their marriage that the Jews plotted and tried to kill the Prophet on more than one occasion, without success, and were punished for this. First the Banu Qaynuqa and then the Banu Nadir were expelled from Madina; and then the Banu Qurayza – who had broken their agreement with the Muslims during the battle of al-Khandaq and conspired to exterminate all of them – were subjected to the punishment that was decided by the man whom they themselves had chosen to judge their actions, Sa'd ibn Mu'adh. In accordance with the commands contained in their own book, the Torah, all the men were killed – with the exception of four who accepted Islam – and all the women and children were taken as slaves.

It was after this event that another tribe, the Banu al-Mustaliq began to prepare to fight the Muslims, and accordingly the Prophet ﷺ led an army against them. Often when the Prophet went to war, he took one of his wives with him. He did not choose any one in particular, but simply drew lots and took the wife whose name came out. When he went to fight the Banu al-Mustaliq, the lot fell to 'A'isha, and she it was who travelled with him.

'A'isha, who was now thirteen years old, was small, slim and graceful, so that it was difficult for the men who carried her litter to know for certain whether or not she was actually inside it when they lifted it up. On the way back to Madina, after the Banu al-Mustaliq had been subdued, the Muslim army stopped for a rest, but then the Prophet unexpectedly ordered the army to continue the march back.

Unknown to everyone else, 'A'isha had stepped out of her litter for a few minutes and had left the camp, seeking some privacy. On her way back she had noticed that her onyx necklace was missing and so she retraced her steps to try and find it. When she had at last found it and finally returned to the camp, it was to find that everyone had gone. The men who had been carrying her litter had thought she was still in it, and had picked it up, strapped it to the camel and marched on.

'A'isha, who trusted completely in Allah, sat down and waited, hoping that someone would notice her absence and come back for her. Fortunately she did not have long to wait, for a young Muslim man named Safwan ibn al-Mu'attal, who had fallen behind the army after taking a rest, reached the camp during the night and found her lying fast asleep. Safwan immediately recognised her, because he had seen her in the early days before Allah had commanded Muslim women to wear the *hijab*.

"*Inna lillahi wa inna ilayhi raji'un!*" – "Surely we come from Allah and surely to Him we return!" he exclaimed in surprise, waking 'A'isha up with the loudness of his voice. He did not say anything else, and as 'A'isha put the scarf that had fallen off her head while she was asleep back on, Safwan made his camel kneel down close to her so that she could climb up on to it; and then, leading the camel with his hand, he set off on foot after the army, hoping that they would soon catch up with it – which they eventually did later the next morning, since the army had halted for a rest during the hottest part of the day.

Unfortunately some hypocrites who had seen Safwan and 'A'isha arrive alone together began to gossip and spread slander-ous lies about them. Eventually the story reached the Prophet himself ﷺ, and by then the whole community was talking about what might or might not have happened between the two young Muslims. Naturally the *muminun* were certain that nothing bad had happened, but the *munafiqun* thought otherwise and were not afraid to insinuate that this was the case.

As a result of all this gossip, the Prophet ﷺ and his household came under a great strain, and in fact 'A'isha herself fell ill, not because she was aware of what the hypocrites were saying about her, but because the Prophet ﷺ did not seem to care for her as much as he had done before the campaign against the Banu al-Mustaliq. Finally, someone told her what some people were saying. This made 'A'isha even more ill, so with the Prophet's permission, she ﷺ went to stay at the house of her parents.

When she arrived, she said to her mother, Umm Ruman, "Mother! What are the people saying?" She replied, "O my daughter! Do not make too much of the business. By Allah, seldom has there been a woman of beauty with a husband who loves her and who has co-wives but that people say a lot against her." 'A'isha said, "Glory be to Allah! The people have really been saying this?"

'A'isha said, "I spent the entire night until morning unable to stop weeping and could not sleep at all. Morning found me still weeping."

In the meantime, when Safwan was confronted with the allegations that had been made, he replied, "Glory be to Allah! By Allah, I have never removed the veil of any woman!"

Since there had been no revelation to clarify the matter, the Prophet ※ asked Barira, who was 'A'isha's maid servant, if she had seen anything in 'A'isha's behaviour that was at all doubtful.

"By Him who sent you with the truth," she replied, "I have seen nothing wrong with her, other than that she is a young girl and sometimes she falls asleep while she is kneading the dough and a lamb comes along and eats it!"

Some of the Companions who were present scolded Barira and told her to come to the point. "Glory be to Allah!" she replied. "I know as much about her as a jeweller knows about a piece of pure gold!"

The Prophet, may Allah bless him and grant him peace, also asked Zaynab bint Jahsh for her opinion, since he valued it highly.

Although she and 'A'isha were frequently at odds with one another and Zaynab's sister, Hamna, was one of those who were actively gossiping and spreading the rumour, she replied without hesitation: "O Messenger of Allah," she said, "I will not repeat anything that I have not heard with my own ears and seen with my own eyes. By Allah, I find nothing in her but goodness."

The Prophet, ※ then tried to vindicate 'A'isha's honour by calling everyone to the mosque and publicly defending her reputation, but the hypocrites who had started the trouble in the first place only made matters worse, so that arguments broke out all over the mosque, and people had almost come to blows over the matter before the Prophet ※ calmed them down and silenced them.

The Prophet ※ then came to Abu Bakr's house, where 'A'isha had been crying her heart out, and in the presence of her parents he first said the *shahada*, and then continued, "If you are innocent, then Allah Himself will protect your honour, and if by accident there has been a lapse on your part, then seek the forgiveness of Allah and He will pardon you, for when a slave admits a fault and turns to Him in repentance, then Allah also turns and accepts that repentance."

'A'isha ؆ said, "When the Messenger of Allah ؅ finished what he was saying, my tears stopped so that I was not aware of a single tear. I said to my father, 'Answer the Messenger of Allah for me regarding what he has said.' He said, 'By Allah, I do not know what to say to the Messenger of Allah.' I said to my mother, 'Answer the Messenger of Allah for me regarding what he has said.' She said, 'By Allah, I do not know what to say to the Messenger of Allah.'"

'A'isha said, "I am a young girl who does not yet recite much of the Qur'an. By Allah, I know that you have heard this story that people are saying and it has become fixed in yourself and you have believed it. If I were to say to you that I am innocent, you would not believe me. If I were to confess to something to you – and Allah knows that I am innocent – you would believe me. By Allah, I can only say what the father of Yusuf said, '**Patience is beautiful, and Allah is my protection against what you describe.**' (*Qur'an*: 12.18)

'A'isha said, "Then I turned over on my bed, Allah knowing that I was innocent and hoping that Allah would proclaim me innocent. However, by Allah, I did not think that any revelation would be sent down regarding me. I thought too little of myself that something would be said in the Qur'an regarding me, however I hoped that the Messenger of Allah ؅ would have a dream in which Allah would exonerate me."

She had hardly finished speaking when the Prophet ؅ received a direct revelation of some more *ayats* of the Qur'an, and when it was over, he smiled and said, "Do not worry, 'A'isha, for Allah has revealed proof of your innocence."

'A'isha's mother, who had been standing next to her, said, "Get up and thank him."

"By Allah," exclaimed 'A'isha, whose title, *'Siddiqa'*, means 'the truthful one', "I will not thank him and praise him, but rather Allah Who has given the revelation that has protected my honour!"

Then the Prophet ﷺ went to the mosque and recited what had just been sent down:

Surely those who fabricated the lie
are a group from among you.
Do not think it is a bad thing for you;
no, it is good for you.
Every man will receive what he has earned for this sin,
and whoever had the greater part in it
will have a great punishment.

Why did the men and women believers,
when they heard it,
not think good in their selves and say:
'This is clearly a lie'?

Why did they not produce four witnesses?
Since they did not produce witnesses,
they are certainly liars in the sight of Allah.

If it were not for the grace of Allah
and His mercy on you
in this world and in the next world,
an awful doom would have overtaken you
for what you repeated.

Since you received it with your tongues,
and repeated what you did not know anything about
with your mouths,
you thought it was a trifle,
but in the sight of Allah it is serious.

Why, when you heard it,
did you not say:
'It is not for us to repeat this.
Glory be to You (O Allah),
this is a serious rumour.'

Allah warns you to never
repeat anything like this again,
if you are indeed believers.

And Allah makes the signs clear to you;
and Allah is Knowing, Wise.

Surely those who love to spread around slander about
those who believe
will have a painful punishment
in this world and in the next world;
and Allah knows and you do not know.

(Qur'an: 24.11-19)

'A'isha' forgave those who had let themselves be caught up in the slander and in later years would not hear anything bad said against them.

The fact that 'A'isha's honour and reputation had been protected by a revelation from Allah could not be ignored by anyone, and from then on everyone was more aware of her high station with Allah.

It was also during the course of 'A'isha's marriage with the Prophet Muhammad ﷺ that the Muslim community expanded so rapidly that Makka was eventually conquered by the Muslim army, and preparations were made for the first of the many battles that were successfully fought against the Romans and the Persians – after the letters from Muhammad ﷺ inviting Heraclius and Chosroes to embrace Islam and worship Allah alone had been contemptuously ignored.

This extraordinary expansion – even the idea of which would, at the time of Khadija's death have seemed like a wild dream – was heralded, in 6 AH, by the treaty of Hudaybiyya, by virtue of which peace was declared between the Quraysh and the Muslims for ten years, and the right of the Muslims to enter Makka and do *'umra* unharmed was recognised by the Quraysh.

Although the Muslims had to wait for a year before they could do *'umra*, that year was not long in passing, and in the interval the Jews of Khaybar, who like the other Jews around Madina had attempted to destroy the Muslim community by breaking their peace agreements with the Muslims and supporting the idol-worshippers, were fought and defeated.

After the Jews of Khaybar had been defeated, a Jewess managed to serve the Prophet some poisoned meat – which itself informed him that it had been poisoned, so that he only had a small taste of it. Even though one of his Companions who had already eaten some of the meat subsequently died, the Messenger of Allah ﷺ forgave the Jewess and let her go free.

The Jews of Khaybar were permitted to stay on their land provided that they paid a yearly tribute to the Muslims. As a result, some of the Muslims began to grow more wealthy than they had been in the past. Indeed on one occasion, the Prophet's wives, led by 'A'isha and Hafsa, asked him for some money that he did not have – for there was never one night that he lay down to sleep with any money in his possession. The Prophet ﷺ was distressed by this – not because he did not have the money to give to them, but rather because it was this that apparently they desired.

At this time, both Abu Bakr and 'Umar visited him ﷺ and they found the Messenger of Allah seated, surrounded by his wives who were all silent. Abu Bakr said to himself, "By Allah, I will say something to cheer up the Messenger of Allah!" So he said, "Messenger of Allah, if I were to see the daughter of Kharija asking me for money, I would strike her on the neck!" The Messenger of Allah ﷺ smiled and said, "These ones you see around me have asked me for money." So Abu Bakr went to grab 'A'isha and 'Umar went to grab Hafsa, both exclaiming, "Do you ask the Messenger of Allah for something he does not have!" The women said, "By Allah, we would never ask the Messenger of Allah for something he does not have!"

This was not the only marital problem which he ﷺ experienced at this time. There was a great deal of rivalry between some of the wives and also Hafsa had told 'A'isha something which the Prophet ﷺ had told her not to disclose because it was something which would increase the friction between the wives. Some sources say that he had told her that Abu Bakr and 'Umar would rule after him. In any case, he stayed away from them for a whole month, during which many of his Companions began to think either that he was going to divorce them or that he had already done so.

It is related by 'Umar ؓ that he went to visit the Prophet ﷺ, who was staying alone in a small upper room, in order to find out what was happening. First of all he visited his daughter Hafsa, who was weeping, and asked her if the Prophet had divorced his wives. "I don't know," she sobbed. Then he went and asked to see the Prophet. After he had been given permission to enter, 'Umar climbed up the ladder and into the small room:

"I visited the Messenger of Allah ﷺ and he was lying on a mat. I sat down and he drew up his lower garment over him. He had nothing else on, and the mat had left its marks on his sides. I looked around at what stores the Messenger of Allah ﷺ had, and saw only a handful of barley equal to one *sa'* and an equal amount of mimosa leaves in the corner of the room and a tanned leather bag hanging nearby, and I was moved to tears. He ﷺ said,

'Ibn al-Khattab, what is making you cry?' and I replied,

'O Messenger of Allah, how can I not cry? This mat has left marks on your sides and I can only see what I have seen of your stores. Caesar and Chosroes are leading their lives of plenty, while you are the Messenger of Allah, His Chosen One, and look what you have!'

'Ibn al-Khattab,' he answered, 'isn't it enough for you that for us there is the next world, and for them there is this world?'

'Yes,' I said. Then I said, 'O Messenger of Allah, what has happened with your wives? If you have divorced them, then truly Allah is with you, and His angels, Jibril and Mika'il, and Abu Bakr and I and the believers are with you.'

"And seldom had I talked like that and hoped that Allah would testify to the words that I uttered." And so it happened that the *ayats* of choice were revealed:

> **If you both turn to Allah in repentance,**
> **then that is what your hearts desire;**
> **and if you help each other against him,**
> **then surely Allah Himself**
> **is his protector, and Jibril, and the righteous from**
> **among the believers,**
> **and as well as that, the angels will help him.**

> **It may be, if he divorces you,**
> **that his Lord will give him wives**
> **who are better than you, who submit, who believe,**
> **who are devout,**
> **who are repentant, who worship, who fast,**
> **whether they have been previously married**
> **or are virgins.**

(Qur'an: 66.4-5)

In fact the Prophet Muhammad ﷺ never divorced any of his wives, and as we grow more aware about how they lived, may Allah be pleased with all of them, it is clear that they possessed all of the qualities of the women described in the last *ayat*. Perhaps this *ayat* served as a reminder to them, a reminder that they would remember for the rest of their days – which for most of them lasted long after the Prophet's ﷺ death.

Returning to *Sayyiduna* 'Umar's account of his visit to the Prophet ﷺ during the month of separation from his wives, 'Umar then asked, "O Messenger of Allah, have you divorced them?" and he replied, "No." So after talking for a while longer – about how in Makka the men tended to dominate the women, whereas in Madina the women tended to dominate the men, which is what the womenfolk from Makka had learned to do after they had made *hijra* to Madina – 'Umar climbed down and stood at the door of the mosque and called out at the top of his voice:

"The Messenger of Allah ﷺ has not divorced his wives!"

After the month was up, the Prophet Muhammad ﷺ first went to 'A'isha's room. She was delighted to see him, but grew more serious when he said that some *ayats* had been revealed to him which required him to put two options before her. "Do not make a hasty decision," he said, "and consult your parents first." He then recited these verses:

O Prophet, say to your wives:
'If you desire the life of this world and its adornments,
then come, and I will make you content,
and I will release you with a fair release.

But if you desire Allah and His Messenger
and the abode of the next world,
then truly Allah has prepared an immense reward
for those of you who do good.'

(Qur'an: 33.28-29)

"Is there any need to consult my parents?" replied 'A'isha. "Indeed I desire Allah and His Messenger and the abode of the next world." And her response was followed by all of his other wives.

'A'isha ﷺ remained true to her word both during the lifetime of the Prophet ﷺ and afterwards. Once, when the Muslims were favoured with great wealth, she was given a gift of one hundred thousand dirhams. She was fasting when she received the money, and distributed all of it to the poor and needy, even though she had no provisions in her house. Shortly after that, her maid servant said to her, "Couldn't you have bought a dirham's worth of meat with which to break your fast?"

"If I had thought of it," she replied, "I would have done so!"

After a year had passed following the treaty of Hudaybiyya, the Muslims travelled to Makka and they were able to complete all the rites of the *'umra*, doing everything as the Prophet ﷺ did it. In accordance with the terms of the treaty, the Muslims left after three days, when their *'umra* had been completed.

Not long after this, the Prophet ﷺ sent an army of three thousand Muslims northwards to the borders of the Byzantine territories in what is now Palestine to chastise the tribes there for killing the messengers whom he had sent to call them to Islam. The tribes called on the Emperor Heraclius for support, and when the Muslim army arrived at Mu'ta, they found themselves facing an army of two hundred thousand men. Many of the Muslims died as *shahids* on the day of the battle, but thanks to the tactics of Khalid bin Walid, the Greeks withdrew the next day, and so the Muslims were able to return to Madina relatively unscathed.

When news of the battle of Mu'ta finally reached Makka, the Quraysh mistakenly believed that the Muslims had been thoroughly defeated by the Greeks, and decided to renew their opposition to the Prophet ﷺ. In doing so, they deliberately broke the treaty that they had made at Hudaybiyya, by allowing their allies to attack and kill some of the allies of the Muslims who lived near Makka.

Accordingly the Prophet Muhammad ﷺ marched on Makka, at the head of an army of ten thousand Muslims. Despite everyone's fears, he conquered it with hardly a drop of blood being spilled. As always, the mercy and forgiveness that he displayed towards those who had relentlessly opposed him for so many years changed peoples' hearts, and many of the people of Makka now embraced Islam as a result.

Having pardoned all of the Quraysh, with the exception of four men who had all committed murder for personal reasons, the Prophet ﷺ smashed all the idols and destroyed all the paintings that had been placed inside the Ka'ba by the idol-worshippers. The sanctity of the sanctuary of Makka had been restored, and at long last the Muslims were free to come and go in Makka as they pleased.

In the midst of the peace and rejoicing, however, news came that the tribes of Hawazin and Thaqif were preparing to attack the Muslims. The Muslim army that had conquered Makka, swelled to twelve thousand by some of the men from the Quraysh who had just embraced Islam, marched to a place called Hunayn.

For the first time in their experience, the Muslims actually outnumbered the enemy, of whom there were only about four thousand.

This nearly proved to be the Muslims' undoing, for many of them felt secure because of their large numbers, rather than because of their reliance on Allah. When the enemy suddenly attacked at dawn, showering down arrows from the hills, the Muslims were taken by surprise and many began to flee.

A small group stood firm with the Prophet ﷺ, one of whom was Umm Sulaym bint Milhan, the wife of Abu Talha. Although she was very pregnant at the time, she had armed herself with a dagger to use against the *kafirun*.

Fortunately the strong Muslims rallied round the Prophet ﷺ, and although there were only six hundred of them, their concerted effort, fighting valiantly in the way of Allah, turned the tide of the battle until those who had turned away in the initial panic and confusion had returned and the battle was won.

After the battle of Hunayn, the only continued resistance to the Muslims was from the north and north-east, from the Byzantine and Persian Empires. Having heard that the Greeks were preparing a huge army to conquer the Muslims, Muhammad ﷺ prepared a large army of thirty thousand men and marched out in the heat of the late summer to do battle with them.

After a long, hard, hot march, the Muslim army reached Tabuk, and here they learned that the Greeks had retreated back into their own territory. Accordingly, having made peace treaties with all the border tribes, the Muslims returned to Madina, in time for many of them to go on the pilgrimage to Makka. Those who had made weak excuses in order to avoid going on the expedition to Tabuk now felt great shame and regret.

The Prophet ﷺ himself did not go on the pilgrimage this year, for people were coming to Madina from all over the Arab lands to embrace Islam and to pledge allegiance to him. It was this year that came to be known as 'the Year of the Delegations', during which, at one point, the Prophet became so exhausted from seeing people that he had to pray sitting down.

So instead, Abu Bakr ؓ led the pilgrims. It was during this *hajj* that the *ayat* in the Qur'an that forbade the idol-worshippers from ever entering the sanctuary of Makka again were revealed; they were made public during the *hajj* by 'Ali ibn Abi Talib ؓ, who was sent straight from Madina to Makka as soon as they had been revealed, so that as many people as possible would hear them.

The following year, when the time for the pilgrimage drew near, the Prophet ﷺ announced that he was going on the *hajj*, and as a result everyone wanted to do it with him. The Muslims who did not live in or near Madina either first travelled to Madina in order to accompany him on the journey to Makka, or else travelled to Makka from every part of Arabia and joined him there.

Amongst the people on what has become known as 'the Farewell Pilgrimage' of the Prophet ﷺ was 'A'isha, for the Prophet asked all of his wives, may Allah be pleased with them, to accompany him, to ensure that they all fulfilled this particular obligation that every Muslim owes to his or her Lord.

It was an extraordinary pilgrimage. There never had been, and there never has been, and there never will be, another *hajj* quite like it, for at its heart was the Prophet Muhammad ﷺ and around him were his Family and Companions, may the blessings and peace of Allah be on them, and during it the *ayat* of the Qur'an was revealed:

> **This day I have perfected your *deen* for you**
> **and have completed My blessing on you,**
> **and have chosen Islam for you as your *deen*.**

(Qur'an: 5.3).

It was also during this *hajj* that the Prophet ﷺ gave his famous Farewell *Khutba*, whose words still ring in our ears and echo in our hearts all these centuries later. When he ﷺ had finished speaking to the thousands upon thousands of Muslims who were gathered around him on the plain of Arafat, he raised his voice slightly and asked, "My Lord, have I delivered the message?"

And thousands upon thousands of voices from all around him answered his question: "Yes, you have." And many of those who were present passed on that message to those who were not present, and so it has continued, right up until today.

And one of those who was present was 'A'isha ﷺ, of whom the Prophet ﷺ once said, may Allah bless him and grant him peace, "Learn some of your *deen* from this red-haired lady," – meaning 'A'isha.

This is not surprising, for she is one of the four people who have transmitted more than two thousand *hadiths*, the others being Abu Hurayra ⁕, 'Abdullah ibn 'Umar ⁕, and Anas ibn Malik ⁕. Many of these *hadiths* are about some of the most intimate aspects of personal behaviour and hygiene which only someone in 'A'isha's position could have learned.

It was during the course of his marriage with 'A'isha ⁕ that the Prophet ⁕ married several other wives, usually to strengthen ties between important families and tribes, or to relieve the hardship of a woman who had been unexpectedly divorced or widowed, or in order to clearly demonstrate whom it was permissible for a Muslim to marry, but above all because all of his marriages had been decreed by Allah, and because all of his wives were exceptional women.

Hafsa bint 'Umar

Hafsa, may Allah be pleased with her, was the daughter of 'Umar ibn al-Khattab ﷺ. She had been married to someone else, but was widowed when she was still very young, only eighteen. 'Umar asked both Abu Bakr and 'Uthman ibn 'Affan, one after the other, if they would like to marry her, but they both declined because they knew that the Prophet ﷺ had expressed an interest in marrying her.

When 'Umar went to the Prophet ﷺ to complain about their behaviour, the Prophet smiled and said, "Hafsa will marry one better than 'Uthman and 'Uthman will marry one better than Hafsa." 'Umar was startled and then realised that it was the Prophet ﷺ who was asking for her hand in marriage. He was overcome with delight. They were married just after the battle of Badr, when Hafsa was about twenty years old and the Prophet ﷺ was fifty-six.

By this marriage, the Prophet ﷺ strengthened the ties between two of his closest companions, the two who would become the first two rightly guided khalifs after his death. He ﷺ was now married to the daughter of *Sayyiduna* Abu Bakr, 'A'isha, and to the daughter of *Sayyiduna* 'Umar, Hafsa.

Two of the other closest companions of the Prophet ﷺ who would become the third and fourth rightly guided khalifs were also connected to the Prophet through marriage:

Sayyiduna 'Uthman ibn 'Affan ﷺ had married Ruqayya, the daughter of the Prophet, in Makka, and then, after her death in Madina soon after the battle of Badr, he had married Umm Kulthum, also the daughter of the Prophet ﷺ. It was because he married two of the daughters of the Prophet, may Allah bless him and grant him peace, that 'Uthman ﷺ was given the title of *Dhu'n-Nurayn,* which means 'the possessor of two lights'.

And *Sayyiduna* 'Ali ibn Abi Talib ﷺ had married Fatima, the youngest daughter of the Prophet, shortly before the Prophet ﷺ had married 'A'isha.

Hafsa, like 'A'isha, with whom she became close friends, was never at a loss for words, and was not afraid to argue with the Prophet ﷺ who was content to allow her to say what she thought. One day, while speaking to Hafsa's mother, 'Umar said, "I think I shall do so-and-so." Whereupon his wife replied, "But it would be better if you did such-and-such."

"Are you arguing with me, woman?" said 'Umar, who was a fierce man who did not expect his wives to talk back at him.

"Why not?" she answered. "Your daughter keeps arguing with the Messenger of Allah until she upsets him for the whole day."

'Umar ﷺ immediately put on his cloak and went directly to his daughter's house. "Is it true that you argue with the Messenger of Allah?" he asked.

"Indeed I do," she replied.

'Umar was just about to chastise her for what he considered were bad manners, when the Prophet ﷺ came into the room and would not allow him to even touch her. So 'Umar went round to visit Umm Salama, to whom 'Umar was related, in order to try and influence Hafsa's behaviour through her.

"I wonder at you, Ibn Khattab," she said, after she had listened to him. "You have interfered in everything. Will you now interfere between the Messenger of Allah and his wives?"

Sayyiduna 'Umar ﷺ, when relating this incident, continued, "And she kept on at me until she made me give up much of what I thought proper."

Some sources say that the Prophet ﷺ divorced Hafsa with a single divorce and that 'Umar was heart-broken when this happened and began to throw dust on his head. Then the Prophet took her back after Jibril ﷺ had descended and said to him, "Take Hafsa back. She fasts and prays and she will be your wife in the Garden."

Like 'A'isha, Hafsa ✿ memorised the whole of the Qur'an by heart. The written copy of the Qur'an which was recorded by Zayd ibn Thabit on Abu Bakr's instructions, and which was then given to 'Umar for safekeeping, was then given by 'Umar to Hafsa to look after. When 'Uthman eventually became the khalif, he instructed several written copies of the Qur'an to be made so that they could be sent to the main centres of the now rapidly expanding Muslim empire – and it was the copy in Hafsa's keeping that was used, after it had been meticulously checked for its accuracy by referring to all the other written records of the Qur'an and to all the Muslims who knew the Qur'an by heart.

Hafsa ✿ lived with the Prophet in Madina for eight years, may Allah bless him and grant him peace, and lived on for another thirty-four years after his death, witnessing with joy the victories and expansion of Islam under her father's guidance, and with sorrow the troubles that beset the Muslim community after the murder of 'Uthman. She died in 47 AH at the age of sixty-three, may Allah be pleased with her.

Zaynab bint Khuzayma

Zaynab bint Khuzayma, may Allah be pleased with her, was married to the Prophet ﷺ in Ramadan, 4 AH, soon after his marriage to Hafsa when he was fifty-six years old and she was thirty years old. After she had been made a widow when her husband was martyred at Badr, she offered herself in marriage to the Prophet ﷺ who accepted her proposal and married her.

Zaynab bint Khuzayma ؓ was so generous to orphans and the poor that she came to be known as the 'Mother of the Poor'. She died only eight months after her marriage, may Allah be pleased with her, and although not a great deal is known about her today, there will be many who will testify to her generosity on the Last Day.

Umm Salama Hind bint Abi Umayya

Umm Salama Hind bint Abi Umayya, may Allah be pleased with her, was married to the Prophet ﷺ in 4 AH at the age of twenty-nine, after her first husband, 'Abdullah ibn 'Abd'al-Asad, had died from the wounds he had received while fighting at the battle of Uhud.

Umm Salama and 'Abd'al-Asad had been among the first people to embrace Islam in the early days of the Muslim community in Makka. They had suffered at the hands of the Quraysh who had tried to force them to abandon their new faith, and had been among the first group of Muslims to seek refuge under the protection of the Negus in Abyssinia.

When they had returned to Makka, believing that the situation of the Muslims had improved, they had found instead that if anything it was worse. Rather than return to Abyssinia, 'Abd'al-Asad and Umm Salama had received the Prophet's permission to emigrate to Madina, but this proved not to be as easy as they might have imagined.

In the words of Umm Salama:

"When Abu Salama (my husband) decided to leave for Madina, he prepared a camel for me, lifted me up onto it and put my son Salama on my lap. My husband then took the lead and went straight ahead without stopping or waiting for anything. Before we were out of Makka, however, some men from my tribe, the Banu Makhzum, stopped us and said to my husband:

"'Although you may be free to do what you like with your self, you have no power over your wife. She is our daughter. Do you expect us to allow you to take her away from us?'

"They then grabbed hold of him and snatched me away from him. Some men from my husband's tribe, the Banu 'Abd'al-

Asad, saw them taking both me and my child, and became hot with rage:

"'No, by Allah!' they shouted. 'We shall not abandon the boy. He is our son and we have a rightful claim over him.' So they took him by his arm and pulled him away from me.

"Suddenly, in the space of a few minutes, I found myself all alone. My husband headed out towards Madina by himself; his tribe had snatched away my son from me; and my own tribe had overpowered me and forced me to stay with them.

"From the day that my husband and my son were parted from me, I went out at noon every day and sat at the spot where this tragedy had occurred. I would remember those terrifying moments and weep until nightfall.

"I continued like this for a year or so until one day a man from the Banu Umayya passed by and saw my condition. He went back to my tribe and said, 'Why don't you free this poor woman? You have caused both her husband and her son to be taken away from her.'

"He went on like this, trying to soften their hearts and appealing to their emotions, until at last they said to me, 'Go and join your husband if you wish.'

"But how could I join my husband in Madina, and leave my son, part of my own flesh and blood, in Makka among the Banu 'Abd'al-Asad? How could I remain free from anguish, and my eyes free from tears, if I were to reach the place of *hijra* not knowing anything of my little son left behind in Makka?

"Some people realised what I was going through and their hearts went out to me. They approached the Banu 'Abd'al-Asad on my behalf and persuaded them to return my son.

"I had no desire to remain in Makka until I could find some-one to travel with me, for I was afraid that something might happen that would delay me or stop me from reaching my husband. So I immediately prepared my camel, placed my son on my lap and set out in the direction of Madina.

"I had just reached Tan'im (about three miles from Mak when I met 'Uthman ibn Talha. (He was in charge of looking after the Ka'ba, but did not embrace Islam until the Conquest of Makka).

"'Where are you going, Bint Zad ar-Rakib?' he asked.

"'I am going to my husband in Madina.'

"'And isn't there anyone going with you?'

"'No, by Allah, except Allah and my little boy here.'

"'By Allah,' he vowed, 'I will not leave you until you reach Madina.'

"He then took the reins of my camel and led us on our way. By Allah, I have never met an Arab more generous and noble than he. Whenever we reached a resting place, he would make my camel kneel down, wait until I had dismounted and then lead the camel to a tree and tether it. Then he would go and rest in the shade of a different tree to me. When we had rested, he would get the camel ready again and then lead us on our way.

"This he did every day until we reached Madina. When we reached a village near Quba (about two miles from Madina), belonging to the Banu 'Amr ibn 'Awf, he said, 'Your husband is in this village. Enter it with the blessings of Allah.'

"Then he turned round and headed back to Makka."

Thus after many difficult months of separation, Umm Salama and her son were reunited with Abu Salama, and in the next few years that followed, they were always near the heart of the growing Muslim community of Madina al-Munawarra. They were present when the Prophet ﷺ and Abu Bakr ؓ arrived safely from Makka, and at the battle of Badr Abu Salama fought bravely.

At the battle of Uhud, however, he was badly wounded. At first his wounds appeared to respond well to treatment, but then his wounds re-opened after an expedition against the Banu 'Abd'al-Asad, and after that they refused to heal and he remained bedridden.

Once while Umm Salama was nursing him, he said to her, "I once heard the Messenger of Allah ﷺ say that whenever a calamity afflicts anyone he should say what Allah has commanded him to say: *'Inna lillahi wa inna ilayhi raji'un!'* – 'Surely we come from Allah and surely to Him we return!' and then he should say, 'O Lord, reward me for my affliction and give me something better than it in return, which only You, the Exalted and Mighty, can give.'"

Abu Salama remained sick in bed for several days. One morning the Prophet ﷺ came to see him. The visit was longer than usual, and while the Prophet was still at his bedside, Abu Salama died. With his blessed hands, the Prophet closed the eyes of his dead Companion and then raised them in prayer:

"O Allah, grant forgiveness to Abu Salama; elevate him among those who are near to You; take charge of his family at all times; forgive us and him, O Lord of the worlds; make his grave spacious for him and fill it with light. Amin."

Once again Umm Salama was alone, only now she had not one child, but several. There was no one to look after her and them. Recalling what her husband had told her while she was looking after him, she repeated the *du'a* that he had remembered: "*Inna lillahi wa inna ilayhi raji'un!*" – "Surely we come from Allah and surely to Him we return!" she repeated. "O Lord, reward me for my affliction and give me something better than it in return, which only You, the Exalted and Mighty, can give."

Then she thought to herself, "What Muslim is better than Abu Salama whose family was the first to emigrate to the Messenger of Allah ﷺ?"

All the Muslims in Madina were aware of Umm Salama's situation, and when her *'idda* period of four months and ten days was over, Abu Bakr ﷺ proposed marriage to her, but she refused. Then 'Umar ﷺ asked her to marry him, but again she refused. Then the Prophet ﷺ himself asked for her hand in marriage.

"O Messenger of Allah," Umm Salama replied, "I have three main characteristics: I am a woman who is extremely jealous and I am afraid that you will see something in me that will make you angry and cause Allah to punish me; I am a woman who is already advanced in age; and I am a woman who has many children."

"As for your jealousy," answered the Prophet 鬱, "I pray to Allah the Almighty to take it away from you. As for your age, I am older than you. As for your many children, they belong to Allah and His Messenger."

The Prophet's answers eased her heart, and so they were married in Shawwal, 4 AH, and so it was that Allah answered the prayer of Umm Salama and gave her better than Abu Salama 緣. From that day on, Umm Salama was not only the mother of Salama, but also became 'the Mother of the Believers' – '*Umm al-Muminin*'.

Umm Salama was not the only wife to have been widowed as a result of the battle of Uhud, and thanks to this marriage, many of the Companions followed the Prophet's example, marrying widows and thereby bringing them and their children into the circle of their families, instead of leaving them to struggle on their own.

'A'isha said, "When the Messenger of Allah 鬱 married Umm Salama, I felt very unhappy when he mentioned her beauty to us. I waited until I saw her and she was even more beautiful than her description." She was also from a very noble family and known for her keen intelligence. On more than one occasion, the Prophet 鬱 asked her advice in tricky situations.

Like 'A'isha and Hafsa, Umm Salama learned the whole of the Qur'an by heart, and an indication of her high station with Allah can be found in the fact that she was permitted to see the angel Jibril 鬱 in human form:

It has been related by Salman that Jibril 鬱, came to the Messenger of Allah 鬱 while Umm Salama was with him, and had a conversation with him. After Jibril had left, the Prophet ﷺ said to Umm Salama, "Do you know who that was?" and she replied that it was a man called Dihya al-Kalbi.

"By Allah," said Umm Salama, "I didn't think it was anyone else until the Messenger of Allah ﷺ told me who it really was."

She also had a home for her four children, Salama, 'Umar, Zaynab and Durra who were the foster children of the Prophet.

Once she was with the Prophet ﷺ with her daughter Zaynab when Fatima came with al-Hasan and al-Husayn. He ﷺ embraced his two grandsons and said, "May the mercy and blessing of Allah be upon you, O People of the House. He is Praiseworthy, Glorious." Umm Salama began to weep and the Messenger of Allah ﷺ looked at her and asked tenderly, "Why are you weeping?"

She replied, " O Messenger of Allah, you singled them out and left out me and my daughter!"

He said, "You and your daughter are among the People of the House."

Her daughter Zaynab grew up in the care of the Messenger ﷺ and became one of the most intelligent women of her time.

Once Zaynab came in while the Prophet was bathing and he splashed water in her face. Afterwards her face retained its youthfulness even into her old age.

Her son Salama later married Umama, the daughter of Hamza, the uncle of the Prophet ﷺ martyred at Uhud.

Umm Salama ◈ was married to the Prophet ﷺ for seven years, until his death in 10 AH, and accompanied him on many of his expeditions: Hudaybiyya, Khaybar, the Conquest of Makka, the siege of Ta'if, the expedition against Hawazin and Thaqif, and the Farewell *Hajj*.

She continued to live for a long time, outliving all the other wives of the Prophet, may Allah be pleased with them, until she died in 61 AH, at the age of eighty-four, may Allah be pleased with her, and Abu Hurayra ◈ said the funeral prayer over her.

Zaynab bint Jahsh

Zaynab bint Jahsh, may Allah be pleased with her, married the Prophet Muhammad ﷺ in 5 AH, when she was thirty-five and the Prophet was fifty-eight, but only after her previous marriage, which had been arranged by the Prophet himself, had ended in divorce. As with all the marriages of the Prophet Muhammad ﷺ, there was much for all the Muslims to learn from it.

Zaynab bint Jahsh was the Prophet Muhammad's cousin, her mother Umayma being the daughter of 'Abd'ul-Muttalib, Muhammad's grandfather, who, while he was alive, had ensured the safety of his grandson, thanks to his position as one of the most respected leaders of the Quraysh. Thus Zaynab bint Jahsh came from one of the noblest families of the Quraysh, and everyone expected her to eventually marry a man with the same high social status.

The Prophet ﷺ was well aware that it is a person's standing in the eyes of Allah that is important, rather than his or her status in the eyes of people. He wanted her to marry a young man called Zayd ibn Harith, whose background was very different to that of Zaynab bint Jahsh.

Zayd had been taken prisoner while he was still a child during one of the inter-tribal wars that had been common before the coming of Islam. He had been sold as a slave to a nephew of Khadija ؓ who had given Zayd to her as a gift. In turn, Khadija had given him to the Prophet Muhammad ﷺ, in the days before the revelation of the Qur'an had begun, and the Prophet, may Allah bless him and grant him peace, had given him his freedom and adopted him as his own son, at the age of eight.

The Prophet Muhammad ﷺ had watched both Zayd and Zaynab grow up, and thought that they would make a good couple, and that their marriage would demonstrate that it was not who their ancestors were, but rather their standing in the sight of Allah, that mattered.

When the Prophet ﷺ asked for her hand on behalf of Zayd, Zaynab and her family were shocked at the idea of her marrying a man who in their eyes was only a freed slave. Moreover, Zaynab wanted to marry the Prophet ﷺ himself and in fact he had already been asked by her family whether or not he would like to marry her. At first both she and her brother refused, but then the following *ayat* was revealed:

It is not for a believing man or a believing woman,
when a matter has been decided
by Allah and His Messenger,
to have any say in their decision;
and whoever disobeys Allah and His Messenger
has most clearly gone astray.

(Qur'an: 33.36)

When Zayd, who also had misgivings about the proposed match, and Zaynab realised that there was no difference between what the Prophet ﷺ wanted and what Allah wanted, they both agreed to the marriage, the Prophet providing a handsome dowry for Zaynab on Zayd's behalf.

The marriage, however, was not a success. Although both Zayd and Zaynab were the best of people, who loved Allah and His Messenger ﷺ, they were very different and in the end they could not overcome their incompatibility. Zayd asked the Prophet's permission to divorce Zaynab more than once, and although he was counselled to hold on to his wife and to fear Allah, in the end the divorce took place.

The Prophet ﷺ was then ordered by Allah to marry Zaynab bint Jahsh ﷺ, which he did in 5 AH, when he was fifty-eight years old and she was thirty-five. In so doing, he demonstrated beyond doubt that in Islam an adopted son is not regarded in the same light as a natural son, and that although a father may never marry a woman whom his natural son has married and then divorced, the father of an adopted son is permitted to marry a woman who was once, but is no longer, married to that adopted son.

Furthermore, by marrying Zaynab, the Prophet ﷺ also confirmed that it is permissible for cousins to marry, and, at the same time, Zaynab ؤ was given her heart's desire to be married to the Best of Creation.

The Messenger of Allah ﷺ received the command to marry Zaynab while he was with 'A'isha ؤ. After he had received the revelation, he smiled and said, "Who will go and give Zaynab the good news?" and he recited the *ayat* that he had received. Some say that it was Zayd himself who took her the good news. When Zaynab heard the news, she stopped what she was doing and prayed to thank Allah. Afterwards, she was fond of pointing out that her marriage had been arranged by Allah.

Zaynab's wedding feast was also the occasion for another *ayat* of Qur'an to be sent down. The Prophet ﷺ sacrificed a sheep and then commanded his servant, Anas, to invite the people to partake of it. After they had eaten, two men remained there after the meal chatting. The Messenger of Allah went out and said good-night to his other wives and then came back and the two men were still there chatting. It was very hard on the Prophet who did not like to criticise people directly, and so he waited patiently until they left. Then Allah sent down the following *ayat* which is known as 'the *Ayat* of the *Hijab*':

O you who believe!
Do not go into the Prophet's rooms
Except after being given permission to come and eat,
not waiting for the food to be prepared.
However, when you are called, then go in
and when you have eaten, then disperse,
and do not remain wanting to chat together.

If you do that, it causes injury to the Prophet
though he is too reticent to tell you.
But Allah is not reticent with the truth.
When you ask his wives for something,
ask them from behind a screen.
That is purer for your hearts and their hearts.
It is not for you to cause injury
to the Messenger of Allah,
nor ever to marry his wives after him.
To do that would be something dreadful
in the sight of Allah.

Whether you make something known or conceal it,
Allah has knowledge of all things.

There is no blame on them regarding
their fathers or their sons or their brothers,
or their brothers' sons or their sisters' sons
or their women or those their right hands own.
Have fear of Allah.
Allah is witness over everything.

Allah and His angels pray blessings on the Prophet.
O you who believe!
Pray blessings on him and ask for peace for him.

(*Qur'an*: 33.53-56)

Zaynab ☙ was a woman who was constantly immersed in the worship of Allah. It is related by Anas ibn Malik that once the Prophet ☙ entered the mosque and found a rope hanging down between two of the pillars, so he said, "What is this?" He was told, "It is for Zaynab. She prays, and when she loses concentration or feels tired, she holds onto it." At this the Prophet ☙ said, "Untie it. Pray as long as you feel fresh, but when you lose concentration or become tired, you should stop."

Zaynab bint Jahsh, like Zaynab bint Khuzayma before her, was very generous to the poor, and indeed the Prophet said, when speaking of her to his other wives, "She is the most generous among you."

Zaynab bint Jahsh ﷺ was with the Prophet ﷺ for six years, and lived for another nine years after his death, dying at the age of fifty, in 20 AH, and thus fulfilling the Prophet's indication that she would be the first of his wives to die after him:

It has been related by 'A'isha ﷺ that the Prophet, ﷺ once said to his wives, "The one who has the longest hands among you will meet me again the soonest."

'A'isha added, "They used to measure each other's hands to see whose was longest, and it was the hand of Zaynab that was the longest, because she used to work by hand and give away (what she earned) in charity."

The Messenger of Allah ﷺ said to 'Umar, "Zaynab bint Jahsh is one who is full of prayer." A man said, "Messenger of Allah, what is that?" He said, "The one who is humble and earnest in prayer."

'A'isha also said of Zaynab, "I have never seen a woman so pure as Zaynab, so God-fearing, so truthful, so attentive to family ties, so generous, so self-sacrificing in everyday life, so charitable, and thus so close to Allah, the Exalted."

Several years after the Prophet ﷺ had died, when *Sayyiduna* 'Umar was the khalif, great wealth came to the Muslims as a result of their victories in fighting the Persians. The treasures of Chosroes, the Persian Emperor, fell into their hands, and when 'Umar ﷺ sent Zaynab a pile of gold as her share of the treasure, she called her maid servant and told her to take a handful of it to so-and-so, naming one of the poor people of Madina.

One after another, she named all the poor people whom she knew, until they had all received a share of the treasure. Then she told her maid servant to see what was left. All that remained of the large pile of gold was eighty dinars, and this she ﷺ accepted as her share, thanking Allah for it; but, because she believed so much money was a temptation, she asked Allah that she would never witness such a large distribution of wealth again.

By the time a year had passed, when 'Umar again came to distribute money amongst those wives of the Prophet who were still alive, her prayer had been granted, for she ﷺ had already passed away, may Allah be pleased with her.

Juwayriyya bint al-Harith

Juwayriyya bint Harith, may Allah be pleased with her, married the Prophet Muhammad, may Allah bless him and grant him peace, in 5 AH, when the Prophet was fifty-eight years old and she was twenty, not long after his marriage to Zaynab bint Jahsh, and as a result of the Muslims' successful campaign against the Banu Mustaliq who were swiftly defeated after the Prophet's surprise attack.

Among the captives taken in this campaign was the beautiful Juwayriyya, the daughter of al-Harith, who was the chief of the Banu Mustaliq. She was afraid that once the Muslims realised who she was, they would demand an exorbitant ransom for her safe release. After the Muslims had returned to Madina with their booty and prisoners, she demanded to see the Prophet Muhammad ﷺ, hoping that he would help to prevent what she feared. Seeing how beautiful she was, 'A'isha was not keen on her seeing the Prophet.

But she persisted, and eventually she was permitted to see the Prophet ﷺ, and was taken to him while he was with 'A'isha. After she had finished speaking, the Prophet ﷺ thought for a moment, may Allah bless him and grant him peace, and then said, "Shall I tell you what would be better than this?"

He ﷺ then asked her to marry him, and she immediately accepted. Although Juwayriyya was young and beautiful and of noble lineage, the Prophet Muhammad ﷺ was thinking of how to save her and all her tribe from an ignoble fate. By marrying Juwayriyya, the Banu Mustaliq would be able to enter Islam with honour, and with the humiliation of their recent defeat removed, so that it would no longer be felt necessary by them to embark on a war of vengeance that would have to continue until one of the two parties had been annihilated.

As soon as the marriage was announced, all the booty that had been taken from the Banu Mustaliq was returned, and all the captives were set free, for they were now the 'in-laws' of the Prophet Muhammad. Thus 'A'isha once said of Juwayriyya, "I know of no woman who was more of a blessing to her people than Juwayriyya bint al-Harith."

After they were married, the Prophet ﷺ changed her name from Barra to Juwayriyya.

It has been related by Juwayriyya ؓ that early one morning the Messenger of Allah ﷺ left her room while she was doing the dawn prayer. He returned later that morning and she was still sitting in the same place. "Have you been sitting in the same place since I left you?" he asked.

"Yes," she replied.

Whereupon the Prophet ﷺ said, "I recited four phrases three times after I left you, and if these were to be weighed against what you have been reciting since dawn, they would still outweigh them. They are: 'Glory be to Allah and Praise be to Him as much as the number of His creations, and His pleasure, and the weight of His Throne, and the ink of His words.'"

Which reminds us of the following *ayat* of the Qur'an:

**Say: 'If the sea were the ink for the words of My Lord,
truly the sea would be used up
before the words of my Lord were completed,
and even if We used the same again to assist.'**

(Qur'an: 18.109)

Juwayriyya ؓ was married to the Prophet ﷺ for six years, and lived for another thirty-nine years after his death, dying in 50 AH at the age of sixty-five, may Allah be pleased with her.

Umm Habiba Ramla bint Abu Sufyan

Umm Habiba Ramla bint Abu Sufyan, may Allah be pleased with her, in fact married the Prophet Muhammad, may Allah bless him and grant him peace, in 1 AH, although she did not actually come to live with him in Madina until 7 AH, when the Prophet ﷺ was sixty years old and she was thirty-five.

Umm Habiba was the daughter of Abu Sufyan, who for some of his life was one of the most resolute enemies of the Prophet ﷺ, spending much of his great wealth in opposing the Muslims, and leading the armies of the *kafirun* against the Muslims in all the early major battles, including the battles of Badr, Uhud and al-Khandaq. Indeed it was not until the conquest of Makka, when the Prophet generously pardoned him, that Abu Sufyan embraced Islam and began to fight with the Muslims instead of against them.

Umm Habiba and her first husband, who was called 'Ubaydullah ibn Jahsh, the brother of Zaynab bint Jahsh, were among the first people to embrace Islam in Makka, and they were among those early Muslims who emigrated to Abyssinia in order to be safe. Once in Abyssinia, however, 'Ubaydullah abandoned Islam and became a Christian. He tried to make her become Christian, but she stood fast. This put Umm Habiba in a difficult position, since a Muslim woman can only be married to a Muslim man. She could no longer live with her husband, and once they had been divorced, she could not return to her father, who was still busy fighting the Muslims.

So she remained with her daughter in Abyssinia, living a very simple life in isolation, waiting to see what Allah would decree for her.

One day, as Umm Habiba sat in her solitary room, a stranger in a strange land far from her home, a maid servant knocked on her door and said that she had been sent by the Negus who had a message for her.

The message was that the Prophet Muhammad ﷺ had asked for her hand in marriage, and that if she accepted this proposal then she was to name one of the Muslims in Abyssinia as her *wakil*, so that the marriage ceremony could take place in Abyssinia even though she was not in the same place as the Prophet ﷺ.

Naturally Umm Habiba was overjoyed and accepted immediately. "Allah has given you good news! Allah has given you good news!" she cried, pulling off what little jewellery she had and giving it to the smiling girl. She asked her to repeat the message three times since she could hardly believe her ears.

Soon after this, all the Muslims who had sought refuge in Abyssinia were summoned to the palace of the Negus to witness the simple marriage ceremony in which the marriage contract was made between the Negus, acting on the Prophet's behalf and her *wakil*, Khalid ibn Sa'id ibn al-'As, acting on her behalf. When the marriage was finalised, the Negus addressed the gathering with these words:

"I praise Allah, the Holy, and I declare that there is no god but Allah and that Muhammad is His servant and His messenger and that He gave the good news to Jesus the son of Mary.

"The Messenger of Allah ﷺ requested me to conclude the marriage contract between him and Umm Habiba, the daughter of Abu Sufyan. I agreed to do what he requested, and on his behalf I give her a dowry of four hundred gold dinars."

The Negus handed over the amount to Khalid ibn Sa'id who stood up and said:

"All praise is due to Allah. I praise Him and I seek His help and forgiveness and I turn to Him in repentance. I bear witness that Muhammad is His servant and His Messenger whom He has sent with the *deen* of guidance and truth so that it may prevail over all other religions, however much those who reject dislike this.

"I agreed to do what the Prophet ﷺ requested and acted as the *wakil* on behalf of Umm Habiba, the daughter of Abu Sufyan. May Allah bless His Messenger ﷺ and his wife. Congratulations to Umm Habiba for the goodness which Allah has decreed for her."

Khalid took the dowry and handed it over to Umm Habiba. Thus although she could not travel to Arabia straight away, she was provided for by the Prophet, may Allah bless him and grant him peace, from the moment that they were married.

The Muslims who had witnessed the marriage contract were just about to leave, when the Negus said to them, "Sit down, for it is the practice of the Prophets to serve food at marriages." Joyfully everyone sat down again to eat and celebrate the happy occasion. Umm Habiba especially could hardly believe her good fortune, and she later described how eager she was to share her happiness, saying:

"When I received the money as my dowry, I sent fifty *mithqals* of gold to the servant girl who had first brought me the good news, and I said to her, 'I gave you what I did when you gave me the good news because at that time I did not have any money at all.'

"Shortly afterwards, she came to me and returned the gold. She also produced a case which contained the necklace I had given to her and gave it to me, saying, 'The Negus has instructed me not to take anything from you, and he has commanded the women in his household to present you with gifts of perfume.'

"On the following day, she brought me ambergris, saffron and aloes wood oil and said, 'I have a favour to ask of you.'

"'What is it?' I asked.

"'I have accepted Islam,' she replied, 'and now I follow the *deen* of Muhammad ﷺ. Please convey my greetings of peace to him, and let him know that I believe in Allah and His Prophet. Please do not forget.'"

Six years later, in 7 AH, when the emigrant Muslims in Abyssinia were finally able to return to Arabia, Umm Habiba came to Madina and there the Prophet Muhammad ﷺ, who had just returned victorious from Khaybar, warmly welcomed her. Umm Habiba relates:

"When I met the Prophet ﷺ I told him all about the arrangements that had been made for the marriage, and about my relationship with the girl. I told him that she had become a Muslim and conveyed her greetings of peace to him. He was filled with joy at the news and said, *'Wa 'alayha as-salam wa rahmatullahi wa barakatuhu'* – 'And on her be the peace and the mercy of Allah and His blessing.'"

The strength of Umm Habiba's character can be measured by what happened shortly before the conquest of Makka, when her father, Abu Sufyan, came to Madina after the Quraysh had broken the treaty of Hudaybiyya, in order to try and re-negotiate a fresh settlement with the Prophet Muhammad and the Muslims.

He first went to Umm Habiba's room and was about to sit down on the blanket on which the Prophet ﷺ slept when Umm Habiba, who had not seen her father for over six years, asked him not to sit on it and quickly folded it up and put it away.

"Am I too good for the bed, or is the bed too good for me?" he asked.

"How can the enemy of Islam sit on the bed of the Holy Prophet?" she replied.

It was only after Abu Sufyan had embraced Islam, after the conquest of Makka, and had become the enemy of the enemies of Islam, that Umm Habiba accepted and loved him again as her father. When she received the news that her father and brother Mu'awiya, who later became the Khalif of the Muslims, had become Muslims after the conquest, she fell down in prostration to Allah out of thankfulness.

Like all the wives of the Prophet ﷺ, Umm Habiba ◈ spent much of her time remembering Allah and worshipping Him. She has related that once the Prophet ﷺ said to her, "A house will be built in the Garden for anyone who, in the space of a day and a night, prays twelve voluntary *rak'ats*;" and she added, "I have never stopped doing this since I heard it from the Messenger of Allah ﷺ."

Umm Habiba ◈ spent four years of her life with the Prophet Muhammad ﷺ and lived for another thirty-three years after he had died, dying at the age of seventy-two in 44 AH, may Allah be pleased with her.

Safiyya bint Huyayy

Safiyya bint Huyayy, may Allah be pleased with her, married the Prophet Muhammad, may Allah bless him and grant him peace, in 7 AH, when the Prophet was sixty years old and she was seventeen years old. As in the case of Juwayriyya bint al-Harith, this marriage occurred after one of the Muslim's decisive battles, in this case, the battle of Khaybar.

After the battle of Khaybar in which the Muslims defeated the Jews, two women were brought before the Prophet Muhammad ﷺ by Bilal, the black *mu'adhdhin* of Madina whose beautifully piercing voice constantly called the Muslims to prayer right up until the Prophet's death – after which he ﷺ could not bring himself to call the *adhan* any more, until he was present at the surrender of Jerusalem to the Khalif 'Umar ﷺ in 17 AH.

They had passed by those who had been killed in the fighting. One of the two women was shrieking and screaming and rubbing dust in her hair, while the other was mute with shock.

The silent one was Safiyya, the daughter of Huyayy ibn Akhtab, the chief of the Banu Nadir who had all been expelled from Madina in 4 AH after plotting to kill the Messenger of Allah by dropping a stone on his head as he sat talking with their leaders. The noisy one was Safiyya's cousin. Safiyya could trace her lineage directly back to Harun, the brother of the Prophet Moses, peace be on them.

The Prophet Muhammad ﷺ asked someone to look after the woman who was screaming, and then took off his cloak and placed it over the shoulders of Safiyya, whose husband had been killed in the battle. It was a gesture of pity, but from that moment she was to be honoured and given great respect in the Muslim community.

Then the Prophet ﷺ turned to Bilal and said, "Bilal, has Allah plucked mercy from your heart that you let these two women pass by those of their menfolk who have been killed?"

This was considered a severe reprimand, for the Messenger of Allah ﷺ very rarely criticised the behaviour of those who served him. Anas ibn Malik ﵁, for example, once said, "I served the Messenger of Allah ﷺ for eight years. He never once scolded me for something that I had done or for something that I had not done."

Like Umm Habiba, Safiyya was the daughter of a great chief. The only person who could save her from becoming a slave after having enjoyed such a high position was the Prophet ﷺ. Although her father had planned to assassinate Muhammad ﷺ after the battle of Uhud, and had conspired with the Banu Qurayza to exterminate all the Muslims during the battle of al-Khandaq, it was a characteristic of the Prophet Muhammad, may Allah bless him and grant him peace, that he did not bear any grudges. For those who did wrong, he felt pity rather than anger, and for those who had done no wrong, he had even greater compassion.

The Prophet Muhammad ﷺ invited Safiyya to embrace Islam, which she did, and having given her her freedom, he then married her. Some people may have wondered how it was that Safiyya could accept Islam and marry the Prophet when her father had been his bitter enemy, and when bloody battles had taken place between the Jews and the Muslims. The answer may be found in what she has related of her early life as the daughter of the chief of the Banu Nadir. She said, may Allah be pleased with her:

"I was my father's favourite and also a favourite with my uncle Yasir. They could never see me with one of their children without picking me up. When the Messenger of Allah ﷺ came to Madina, my father and my uncle went to see him. It was very early in the morning, between dawn and sunrise. They did not return until the sun was setting. They came back worn out and depressed, walking with slow, heavy steps. I smiled to them as I always did, but neither of them took any notice of me because they were so miserable. I heard Abu Yasir ask my father, 'Is it him?'

"'Yes, it is.'

"'Can you recognise him? Can you verify it?'

"'Yes, I can recognise him only too well.'

"'What do you feel towards him?'

"'Enmity, enmity as long as I live.'"

The significance of this conversation is evident when we recall that in the Torah of the Jews, it was written that a Prophet would come who would lead those who followed him to victory. Indeed before the Prophet Muhammad ﷺ came to Madina, the Jews used to threaten the idol-worshippers of Yathrib, as it was then called, that when the next Prophet came the believers were going to exterminate them, just as the Jews had exterminated other tribes who refused to worship God in the past.

As in the case of the Prophet Jesus, peace be on him, who had been clearly described in the Torah – but rejected by many of the Jews when he actually came – the next and last Prophet was accurately described in the Torah, which also contained signs by which the Jews could easily recognise him. Thus Ka'b al-Ahbar, one of the Jews of that time who embraced Islam, relates that this Prophet is described in the Torah as follows:

'My slave, Ahmad, the Chosen, born in Makka, who will emigrate to Madina (or he said *Tayyiba* – another name given to Yathrib); his community will be those who praise Allah in every state.'

And 'Amr ibn al-'As said that it also says in the Torah:

'O Prophet, We have sent you as a witness, a bringer of good news and a warner and a refuge for the illiterate. You are My slave and My messenger. I have called you the one on whom people rely, one who is neither coarse nor vulgar, and who neither shouts in the markets nor repays evil with evil, but rather pardons and forgives. Allah will not take him back to Himself until the crooked community has been straightened out by him and they say, "There is no god but Allah." Through him, blind eyes, deaf ears and covered hearts will be opened.'

It was thanks to these descriptions in the Torah, that the most learned rabbi of the Jews, 'Abdullah ibn Salam, had embraced Islam on seeing Muhammad 鸒 and it was because of these descriptions that Huyayy ibn Akhtab was also able to recognise him.

However Huyayy, like most of the other Jews, was deeply disappointed that the last Prophet 鸒 was a descendant of Isma'il and not of Ishaq, (the two sons of the Prophet Ibrahim, peace be on them), since the Jews of that time claimed exclusive descent from Ishaq, through the twelve sons of his son Ya'qub (who was also known as Israel), from whom the twelve tribes of Israel had originated.

Not only did Huyayy resent the fact that the last Prophet had appeared amongst the Arabs, but also he did not want to lose his position of power and leadership over his people.

It was for these reasons that Huyayy secretly decided to oppose and fight the Prophet Muhammad 鸒 – while in public he and the other leaders of the Jews made peace treaties with the Muslims that the Jews repeatedly broke as soon as it seemed a favourable time to do so.

Although Safiyya was Huyayy's daughter, she had a pure heart and had always wanted to worship her Creator and Lord, the One who had sent Moses, to whom she was related, and Jesus, and finally Muhammad, may the blessings and peace of Allah be on them. Thus as soon as the opportunity arose, not only to follow the last Prophet 鸒, but also to be married to him, she took it.

Although Safiyya 🌸 had in Muhammad 🌸 a most kind and considerate husband, she was not always favourably accepted by some of his other wives, especially when she first joined the Prophet's household. It is related by Anas ibn Malik that on one occasion, the Prophet 🌸 found Safiyya weeping. When he asked her what the matter was, she replied that she had heard that Hafsa had disparagingly described her as 'the daughter of a Jew'.

The Prophet 🌸 responded by saying, "You are certainly the daughter of a Prophet [Harun], and certainly your uncle was a Prophet [Moses], and you are certainly the wife of a Prophet [Muhammad], so what is there in that to be scornful towards you?" Then he said to Hafsa, "O Hafsa, fear Allah!"

Once the Prophet 🌸 was accompanied on a journey by Safiyya and Zaynab bint Jahsh when Safiyya's camel went lame. Zaynab had an extra camel and the Prophet 🌸 asked her if she would give it to Safiyya. Zaynab retorted, "Should I give to that Jewess!" The Prophet 🌸 turned away from her in anger and would not have anything to do with her for two or three months to show his disapproval of what she had said.

Some three years later, when Muhammad 🌸 was in his final illness, Safiyya felt for him deeply and sincerely. "O Messenger of Allah," she said, "I wish it was I who was suffering instead of you." Some of the wives winked at each other which made the Prophet cross and he exclaimed, "By Allah, she spoke the truth!"

She still underwent difficulties after the death of the Prophet 🌸. Once a slavegirl she owned went to the Amir al-Muminin 'Umar 🌸 and said, "Amir al-Muminin! Safiyya loves the Sabbath and maintains ties with the Jews!"

'Umar asked Safiyya about that and she said, "I have not loved the Sabbath since Allah replaced it with Friday for me, and I only maintain ties with those Jews to whom I am related by kinship."

She asked her slavegirl what had possessed her to carry lies to 'Umar and the girl replied, "Shaytan!"

Safiyya said, "Go, you are free."

Safiyya ❀ was with the Prophet for nearly four years. She was only twenty-one when the Prophet ❀ died, and lived as a widow for the next thirty-nine years, dying in 50 AH at the age of sixty, may Allah be pleased with her.

Maymuna bint al-Harith

Maymuna bint al-Harith, may Allah be pleased with her, married the Prophet Muhammad, may Allah bless him and grant him peace, in 7 AH, when the Prophet was sixty years old and she was thirty-six years old.

Maymuna's sister, Umm al-Fadl Lubaba, was the mother of 'Abdullah ibn 'Abbas, the son of one of the uncles of the Prophet ﷺ and one of the wisest of his Companions. Umm al-Fadl was one of the earliest Companions of the Prophet. Once Abu Lahab, the enemy of Allah and the Messenger of Allah, entered the house of his brother, al-'Abbas, and proceeded to attack 'Abbas' client, Abu Rafi', because he had embraced Islam. Abu Lahab knocked him to the ground and knelt on him, continuing to beat him. Umm al-Fadl grabbed a post that was there and cracked it across Abu Lahab's head, saying, "Will you victimise him because his master is absent?" He retreated in shame and died a week later.

Zaynab bint Khuzayma, *Umm al-Muminin*, was also her half-sister. Her other sisters included 'Asma' bint 'Umays, the wife of Ja'far ibn Abi Talib, who later married *Sayyiduna* Abu Bakr, and Salma bint 'Umays, the wife of Hamza, the 'Lion of Allah'. Her full sisters were Lubaba, 'Asma' and 'Izza.

Maymuna was thus one of the *'Ahlu'l-Bayt'* – 'the People of the House', not only by virtue of being a wife of the Prophet, may the blessings and peace of Allah be on him and his Family, but also because she was related to him.

Zayd ibn Arqam related that the Messenger of Allah ﷺ said "I implore you by Allah! The People of my House!" three times. Zayd was asked who were the People of the House, and he said, "The family of 'Ali ibn Abi Talib, the family of Ja'far ibn Abi Talib, the family of 'Aqil ibn Abi Talib, and the family of al-'Abbas ibn 'Abdal-Muttalib."

Maymuna, or Barra as she was then called, yearned to marry the Prophet. She went to her sister, Umm al-Fadl, to talk to her about that and she, in turn, spoke to her husband, al-'Abbas. Al-'Abbas immediately went to the Messenger of Allah ﷺ with Maymuna's offer of marriage to him and her proposal was accepted. When the good news reached her, she was on a camel, and she immediately got off the camel and said, "The camel and what is on it is for the Messenger of Allah ﷺ."

They were married in the month of Shawwal in 7 AH just after the Muslims of Madina were permitted to visit Makka under the terms of the treaty of Hudaybiyya, to perform *'umra.* Allah Almighty sent down the following *ayat* about this:

Any believing woman who dedicates
her self to the Prophet
if the Prophet wishes to wed her –
this is only for thee, and not for the believers.

(Qur'an: 33:50)

The Prophet ﷺ gave her the name, Maymuna, meaning "blessed", and Maymuna lived with the Prophet for just over three years, until his death. She was obviously very good-natured and got on well with everyone, and no quarrel or disagreement with any of the Prophet's other wives has been related about her.

'A'isha ؓ said about her, "Among us, she had the most fear of Allah and did the most to maintain ties of kinship."

It was in her room that the Prophet ﷺ first began to feel the effects of what became his final illness and asked the permission of his wives to stay in 'A'isha's room while it lasted.

After the Prophet's death, may Allah fill his grave with peace and light, Maymuna continued to live in Madina for another forty years, dying at the age of eighty, in 51 AH, may Allah be pleased with her. She asked to be buried where she had married the Prophet ﷺ, at Saraf, and her request was carried out. Some sources state that she died in 61 AH, in which case she was the last of the wives of the Prophet ﷺ to die.

It is related that at the funeral of Maymuna, Ibn 'Abbas said, "This is the wife of Allah's Messenger, may Allah bless him and grant him peace, so when you lift her bier, do not shake her or disturb her, but be gentle."

It is also related by Ibn 'Abbas ﷺ that he once stayed the night as a guest of Maymuna, who was his aunt, and the Prophet, may Allah bless him and grant him peace. They slept on their blanket lengthways, and he slept at the end, crossways. After they had all slept for a while, the Prophet ﷺ rose in the middle of the night to pray the *tahajjud* prayer, and Ibn 'Abbas joined him.

They both did *wudu'*, and he prayed eleven *rak'ats* with the Prophet ﷺ. Then they both went back to sleep again until dawn. Bilal ﷺ called the *adhan*, and the Prophet did another two short *rak'ats*, before going into the mosque to lead the Dawn Prayer.

Ibn 'Abbas said that one of the *du'a's* that the Prophet ﷺ made during this night was: "O Allah, place light in my heart, light in my tongue, light in my hearing, light in my sight, light behind me, light in front of me, light on my right, light on my left, light above me and light below me; place light in my sinew, in my flesh, in my blood, in my hair and in my skin; place light in my soul and make light abundant for me; make me light and grant me light."

It is commonly agreed that it was after the Prophet had married Maymuna ﷺ, giving him now nine wives ('A'isha, Sawda, Hafsa, Umm Salama, Zainab bint Jahsh, Juwayriyya, Umm Habiba, Safiyya and Maymuna), that the following *ayat* was revealed:

It is not lawful for you
(O Muhammad, to marry more)
women after this, nor to exchange them
for other wives,

even though their beauty is pleasing to you,
except those whom your right hand possesses
(as maid servants);
and Allah is always watching over everything.

(Qur'an: 33.52)

After this, the Prophet ﷺ did not marry again.

When, however, the Christian ruler, or Muqawqis, of Egypt, sent him two Christian slave-girls – who were sisters – as a gift (in response to the Prophet's letter inviting him to embrace Islam), along with a fine robe and some medicine, the Prophet accepted one of the slave-girls, Maria, into his household; he gave her sister, Serene, to a man whom he wished to honour, namely Hassan ibn Thabit; he accepted the robe; and he returned the medicine with the message, "My *Sunna* is my medicine!" This occurred in 7 AH, when the Prophet ﷺ was sixty years old and Maria was twenty years old.

Maria al-Qibtiyya

Maria al-Qibtiyya, may Allah be pleased with her, is said to have married the Prophet Muhammad, may Allah bless him and grant him peace, and certainly everyone gave her the same title of respect as the Prophet's wives, '*Umm al-Muminin*' – 'Mother of the Believers'.

Maria was born in upper Egypt of a Coptic father and Greek mother and moved to the court of the Muqawqis when she was still very young. She arrived in Madina to join the Prophet's household just after the Prophet ﷺ had returned from making the treaty with the Quraysh which was contracted at al-Hudaybiyya.

Maria gave birth to a healthy son in 9 AH, the same year that his daughter Zaynab died, and the Prophet ﷺ named his new son Ibrahim, after the ancestor of both the Jews and the Christians, the Prophet from whom all the Prophets who came after him were descended, may Allah bless all of them and grant them peace.

Unfortunately, when he was only eighteen months old, Ibrahim became seriously ill and died. Even though he knew that his small son would go to the Garden, the Prophet Muhammad ﷺ could not help shedding some tears. When some of his Companions asked him why he was weeping, he replied, "It is my humanness."

As Ibrahim's body was being buried, the sun was eclipsed and it grew dark and gloomy. Some people thought that this was connected with Ibrahim's death, but the Prophet ﷺ soon clarified this:

"The sun and the moon are two of Allah's signs," he ﷺ said. "They are not eclipsed because of anyone's birth or death. When you see these signs, make haste to remember Allah in prayer."

Although the *kafirun* used to mock the Prophet Muhammad
ﷺ because he had no sons, and say that he was 'cut off', Allah
made it clear in the following *sura* that the station of the Prophet
Muhammad, may Allah bless him and grant him peace, was far
above that of any other man:

In the Name of Allah the Merciful the Compassionate
Surely we have given you Al-Kawthar,
so pray to your Lord
and offer sacrifice.
Surely he who mocks you is the one cut off.

(Qur'an: 108.1-3)

Allah also says in the Qur'an:

Muhammad is not the father of any man among you,
but he is the Messenger of Allah
and the Seal of the Prophets;
and Allah has knowledge of everything.

(Qur'an: 33.40)

Maria ﷢ was honoured and respected by the Prophet ﷺ and
his Family and Companions. She spent three years of her life
with the Prophet, until his death, and died five years later in
16 AH, may Allah be pleased with her. For the last five years
of her life she remained a recluse and almost never went out
except to visit the grave of the Prophet ﷺ or her son's grave.
After her death, 'Umar ibn al-Khattab ﷠ led the prayer over
her and she was buried in al-Baqi'.

The Position of 'A'isha

Of the Prophet's wives in Madina, may Allah be pleased with all of them, it is clear that it was 'A'isha ﴾ that the Messenger of Allah ﷺ loved the most:

From time to time, one or another of his Companions would ask him who it was that he loved the most, and the Prophet, may Allah bless him and grant him peace, did not always give the same answer to this question, for he felt great love for many – for his wives, for his daughters by Khadija, for their children, for *Sayyiduna* Abu Bakr and *Sayyiduna* 'Umar and *Sayyiduna* 'Uthman and *Sayyiduna* 'Ali, and for many of his Companions and community, may Allah be pleased with all of them – but of his wives the only one whom he named in this connection was 'A'isha ﴾.

She too loved him greatly in return and often would seek reassurance from him that he loved her. "How is your love for me?" she once asked.

"Like the rope's knot," he replied, meaning that it was strong and secure.

Many times after that she would ask, "How is the knot?" and he ﷺ would reply:

"*'Ala haliha*" – "The same as always!"

Since 'A'isha loved the Prophet ﷺ so much, she could not help being jealous if his attentions were directed towards others more than what seemed enough to her. She once asked him, "O Messenger of Allah, tell me about yourself. If you were between the two slopes of a valley, one of which had not been grazed, while the other had been grazed, on which slope would you pasture your flocks?"

"On the one that had not been grazed," replied the Prophet, may Allah bless him and grant him peace.

"Even so," she said, "and I am not like any of your other wives. Every one of them had a husband before you, except myself."

The Prophet ﷺ smiled and said nothing.

It is clear that in spite of his wives' high station with Allah, may Allah be pleased with them, they were still human, and at times rather jealous of each other. Thus, for example, it has been related by 'A'isha ؓ that the Prophet ﷺ usually visited his wives every afternoon, after the *'Asr* prayer. On one occasion he stayed longer than usual in the room of Zaynab bint Jahsh, for someone had given her some honey, of which the Prophet ﷺ was very fond.

"At this," said 'A'isha, "I felt jealous, and I, Hafsa, Sawda and Safiyya agreed between ourselves that as he visited each of us, we would tell him that there was a funny smell coming from his mouth from what he had eaten, for we knew that he was particularly sensitive to offensive smells."

Everything went as planned, and as a result, the Prophet ﷺ vowed that he would never eat honey again – only to be reprimanded by the revelation of the following *ayat*:

O Prophet, why do you forbid
what Allah has made lawful for you,
in seeking to please your wives?
And Allah is Forgiving, Compassionate.

(Qur'an: 66.1)

Allah made the whole matter known to the Prophet ﷺ and he confronted the one whose idea it had been with the truth:

So when he told her about it, she said,
'Who told you this?'
He said, 'I was told by the Knowing, the Aware.'

(Qur'an: 66.3)

This incident indicates the extent of the Prophet's submission to Allah. The Prophet ﷺ was the means by which Allah taught the Muslims their *deen* in every moment and situation. What might have seemed an innocent bit of fun to his wives, may Allah be pleased with them, was not permitted by Allah to result in any alteration to the *hudud* of Allah, to what is permitted and what is forbidden by Allah, for if the Prophet ﷺ had never eaten honey again, then many of his Companions and followers might have done likewise.

On another occasion, when one of the Prophet's other wives, Umm Salama ﷺ, complained on their behalf about the fact that more presents were being given to the Prophet on the day that he was with 'A'isha than on the days when he was with his other wives, he ﷺ replied, "O Umm Salama, do not trouble me by harming 'A'isha, for by Allah, the Divine inspiration never came to me while I was under the blanket of any woman amongst you except her."

"I turn to Allah from troubling you, O Messenger of Allah," she said.

However the Prophet's other wives were still not content, and asked Fatima ﷺ to speak to the Prophet on their behalf. When she raised the subject, he said, may Allah bless him and grant him peace, "O my daughter, do you not love those I love?"

"Yes," she said.

"Then love her," he replied.

On another occasion, 'A'isha was on a journey with the Prophet ﷺ and some of his Companions. She had borrowed a necklace from her sister Asma' and during the journey she discovered that she had mislaid it. The journey was delayed while some of the Companions looked for it, and after a while the time for the prayer came. There was no water with which to do *wudu'*, so they became very agitated about that. They went to Abu Bakr ﷺ and said, "Do you see what 'A'isha has done!

She has caused the Messenger of Allah ﷺ to stop at a place where there is no water!"

Meanwhile, the Prophet ﷺ had fallen asleep with his head resting against 'A'isha's leg. Abu Bakr went up to 'A'isha and started to poke her and upbraid her for holding up the people when they did not have any water. She did not move because she did not want to disturb the Prophet's sleep. The Prophet ﷺ soon woke up and the *ayats* about *tayammum* were revealed, making it clear to everyone what should be done when a Muslim on a journey needs to do *wudu'* but has no water.

Usayd ibn Hudayr said to Abu Bakr ﷺ, "This is not the first blessing to have come from your family," and to 'A'isha, " May Allah reward you with good! By Allah, whenever you have a difficulty, Allah relieves you of it and gives a blessing to the Muslims by it as well!"

When they were about to resume their journey, 'A'isha's camel rose to its feet – and there was the necklace. The camel had been lying on it all the time!

Being the daughter of *Sayyiduna* Abu Bakr ﷺ, who on one occasion had given away all his wealth to be spent in the way of Allah, and the wife of Muhammad ﷺ, who kept nothing for himself, 'A'isha ﷺ was very generous. On one occasion, the Prophet had sacrificed an animal, and 'A'isha was so generous in sharing the meat out amongst the poor that she found that she had left nothing for the Messenger's large household except one shoulder of the animal. Feeling a little distressed, she went to Muhammad ﷺ, and said, "I've only been able to save this."

"That is the only part that you have not saved," smiled the Prophet ﷺ, "for whatever you give away in the Name of Allah, you save, and whatever you keep for yourself, you lose."

It is sometimes forgotten that the Prophet Muhammad ﷺ and his wives and Companions, may the blessings and peace of Allah be on him and on his Family and his Companions, led very simple lives. It has been related that sometimes there was no smoke to be seen coming from the Prophet's home for weeks at a time – meaning that there was not even flour to bake bread, let alone meat – so that all there was to eat was dates and water, dates that came from palms whose roots the Prophet ﷺ said were in the Garden.

On another occasion, a beggar asked 'A'isha for some food while she was fasting, and there was only a loaf of bread in her house. She said to her maid servant, "Give it to him."

"But you will not have anything to eat when you break your fast," protested her servant.

"Give it to him," repeated 'A'isha. So she did so.

When evening came, the people of the house of a man who did not usually give to them, gave them a sheep and some food to go with it. 'A'isha called her servant and said, "Eat from this. This is better than your loaf of bread!"

It has been related by 'A'isha ﷺ, that once when it was the Prophet's turn to spend the night with her, he quietly got up towards the end of the night and slipped out of the room, closing the door quietly behind him. 'A'isha was curious to see where he was going, thinking that he had waited until he thought she was asleep. Quickly she got up, covered her head and silently followed him until he came to the graveyard of al-Baqi'.

"He stood there," said 'A'isha, "and he stood for a long time. Then he lifted his hands (in prayer) three times, and then turned to go, so I turned. He quickened his step, so I quickened my step. He began to run, so I began to run. I got back before he did, and entered my room and lay down. He came in and said, 'Why are you out of breath, 'A'isha?'

"'It's nothing,' I said.

"'Tell me, or the One Who is All-Pervading and All-Aware will tell me.'

"'Messenger of Allah,' I said, 'may my father and mother be a ransom for you,' and then I told him.

"'Was it you who I saw running in front of me?' he said.

"'Yes,' I replied, and he hit me on the chest and it hurt.

"'Did you think that Allah and His Messenger would treat you unjustly?' he asked.

"'Whatever anyone conceals, Allah knows it,' I replied.

"'When you saw me leaving,' the Prophet ﷺ explained, 'it was because Jibril had come to me. He called me without you knowing it, and I replied, but without you knowing it, because you were not fully dressed. I thought that you were asleep, and did not want to awaken you in case you were frightened. He (Jibril) said, "Your Lord has commanded you to go to the people of al-Baqi' and to ask forgiveness for them."'

"I said, 'How should I pray for them?'

"'Say: "Peace be on the people of this place (the graveyard), from among the believers and the Muslims, and may Allah have mercy on those who have gone ahead of us, and on those who will follow later; and *insh'Allah* we will join you."'"

As the day of his own death approached, may Allah bless him and grant him peace, it is clear that the Prophet wished to die in the company of 'A'isha, for it is reported that during his final illness, which was probably the result of the poisoned food that he had been given at Khaybar, he enquired, "Where will I be tomorrow, where will I be tomorrow?" since he was hoping it would soon be 'A'isha's turn to be with him. In fact the Prophet ﷺ asked his wives' permission to remain in 'A'isha's room during his illness, and his other wives, may Allah be pleased with them, agreed to forego their turns.

For much of the time during his last few days on earth the Prophet ﷺ lay on a couch with his head resting on 'A'isha's breast or lap. She it was who repeatedly recited the last two *suras* of the Qur'an, the two *suras* of seeking protection, and then blew her breath over him, just as he had taught her to do in the past, and then passed his hand over his body. It is related by 'A'isha that she used his hand rather than her own, because she knew that his hand had greater healing in it than her hand.

She it was who took a toothstick from her brother, chewed it to soften it and then gave it to the Prophet ﷺ. Despite his weakness, he rubbed his teeth with it vigorously. "So," said 'A'isha some time later, "Allah made my saliva mix with his saliva on his last day in this world and his first day in the next world."

Not long afterwards, he ﷺ lost consciousness and 'A'isha thought it was the onset of death, but after a while, he opened his eyes and murmured, "The Highest Company ..." 'A'isha remembered that when the Prophet ﷺ had been in good health in the past, he had said, "No Prophet is taken by death until he has been shown his place in the Garden, and then offered the choice, to remain in this world or to go to the Next World."

Remembering these words, she said to herself, "Then he will not stay with us."

Then she heard him murmur, "O Allah, forgive me and have mercy on me and join me with the Highest Company, **'the people whom Allah has blessed from among the Prophets, and the truthful ones, and the martyrs, and the righteous ones – and the best of company are they.'**" (*Qur'an*: 4.69)

It was then that 'A'isha knew that he ﷺ had been given the choice, and that he had made it.

Again she heard him murmur, "O Allah, with the Highest Company," and these were the last words she heard him speak. Gradually his head grew heavier upon her breast, and gently she laid it on the pillow. Her beloved husband, the Messenger of Allah, the Seal of the Prophets, the Best of Creation, may Allah bless him and grant him peace abundantly, had died in her arms.

At the time of his death, the Prophet Muhammad, may Allah bless him and grant him peace, was sixty-three years old, and 'A'isha ؓ was eighteen.

At first the Prophet's Companions were not sure where he should be buried, but then Abu Bakr as-Siddiq ؓ remembered that while he was alive, the Prophet had said that Prophets were always buried where they had died, so the Prophet ﷺ was buried in 'A'isha's room where he had died.

'A'isha has related that during his final illness, Umm Habiba and Umm Salama mentioned that when they had been in Abyssinia they had seen a church which had pictures in it. The Prophet ﷺ replied, "When one of their righteous people die, they build a place of worship on his grave and then decorate it with such pictures. In the sight of Allah they will be the worst of people on the Day of Judgement."

'A'isha has also related that the Prophet ﷺ said, "Allah has cursed the Jews and the Christians because they made the graves of their Prophets and righteous ones places of worship." 'A'isha continued, "If it had not been for this, his grave would have been in an open place, but it could not be so, due to the fact that it might become a mosque."

In the passage of time, the Prophet's mosque in Madina was enlarged again and again, so that now his grave is no longer next to the mosque, but inside it. Indeed today the extent of the mosque now covers the entire area of what used to be Madina in the time of the Prophet ﷺ. However, although the hearts of the millions of Muslims who visit Madina every year are filled with love for the Messenger of Allah, may Allah bless him and grant him peace, they are always careful to direct their worship towards Allah alone, perhaps remembering the words of *Sayyiduna* Abu Bakr when he first spoke to the Muslims who could not believe that their beloved Prophet had actually died:

"Whoever worshipped Muhammad, Muhammad is dead, and whoever worships Allah – Allah is the Living and does not die."

Then he quoted the *ayat*:

Muhammad is only a Messenger,
whom other messengers have preceded.

**Will it be that when he dies or is killed,
you will turn back on your heels?
And whoever turns back on his heels
will not harm Allah in the least,
and Allah will reward the thankful.**

(Qur'an: 3.144)

Thus it was that the Family and Companions of the Prophet Muhammad, may the blessings and peace of Allah be on him and them, had to accept the inevitable, even though no loss ever had been or ever would be as great as theirs.

It has been related by Anas ibn Malik ☙ that after the death of the Messenger of Allah ☙ *Sayyiduna* Abu Bakr ☙ said to *Sayyiduna* Umar ☙, "Let us visit Umm Ayman [who had looked after the Prophet when he was a small boy], for the Messenger of Allah ☙ used to visit her."

When they came to her ☙, she was weeping, and they said to her: "Why are you weeping? What the Messenger of Allah, may Allah bless him and grant him peace, has now is better than this."

"I am not weeping because I am unaware of the fact that what the Messenger of Allah, may Allah bless him and grant him peace, has now is better than this," she replied, "but I am weeping because the revelation that used to come from the heavens has ceased."

This moved both of them to tears, and they began to weep with her.

'A'isha Siddiqa ☙, who once said, "O would that I were a leaf on a tree!" lived on for another fifty years after the Prophet's death, may Allah bless him and grant him peace, dying at the age of sixty-eight, in 58 AH, may Allah be pleased with her.

During that time she saw many changes, not all of which were pleasant ones, for with the expansion and the conquests that the Muslims experienced, there came wealth, and with the wealth came disagreements and power struggles, and as we all know, the Prophet ﷺ said, "I do not fear poverty for my community, but I fear wealth for them, for it may destroy them as it destroyed the people before them."

'A'isha, however, like all of the Prophet's wives, may Allah be pleased with all of them, remained detached from this world and longed to be re-united with the Prophet ﷺ in the next; but while she was alive, she passed on her knowledge and wisdom to everyone who came to her. Much of what she ﵂ transmitted was recorded in written form, and so countless Muslims have continued to benefit from it right up until today.

Abu Musa reported that Allah's Messenger, may Allah bless him and grant him peace, said, "There have been many men who have reached perfection, but no women have reached perfection except Mary, the daughter of 'Imran, Asiyya, the wife of Pharaoh, and the excellence of 'A'isha as compared to other women is that of *tharid* [meat or vegetable stew, which was the Prophet's favourite food] over all other foods."

Conclusion

Qadi 'Iyad relates that the Prophet said, may Allah bless him and grant him peace, "Recognition of the Family of Muhammad is freedom from the Fire. Love of the Family of Muhammad is crossing over the *Sirat*. Friendship for the Family of Muhammad is safety from the Fire."

One of the *'ulama'* said, "'Recognition' in this case means recognising their place in relation to the Prophet ﷺ. Recognition of that brings with it recognition of the rights and respect that are due to them because of it."

Qadi 'Iyad also wrote:

"Cursing the people of the Prophet's house, his wives and his Companions, and disparaging them is *haram*, and the one who does it is cursed.

'Abdullah ibn Mughaffal said that the Messenger of Allah ﷺ said, "Allah, Allah, my Companions! Do not make them a target after me. Whoever loves them, it is by my love that he loves them. Whoever hates them, incurs my hate by doing so. Whoever harms them has harmed me. Whoever harms me has harmed Allah. Whoever harms Allah is about to be seized." (At-Tirmidhi).

The Messenger of Allah, may Allah bless him and grant him peace, said, "Do not curse my Companions. Whoever curses them, the curse of Allah and the angels and all people is on him. Allah will not accept any recompense or counterweight from him."

The Prophet ﷺ said, "Do not curse my Companions. A people will come at the end of time who will curse my Companions. Do not join them and do not join with them and do not marry with them and do not sit in their assemblies. If they are ill, do not visit them."

The Prophet ﷺ said, "Whoever curses my Companions, beat him."

The Prophet, may Allah bless him and grant him peace, reported that cursing and harming them harmed him. It is *haram* to harm the Prophet ﷺ.

He said, "Do not harm me in respect of 'A'isha."

He said about Fatima, "She is part of me. What harms her harms me."

The best known position with respect to speaking ill of the Companions is that adopted by the school of Malik.

Malik said, "Whoever reviles the Prophet, may Allah bless him and grant him peace, is killed. Whoever reviles his Companions should be disciplined."

Qadi 'Iyad also wrote:

It is related from Malik that anyone who curses Abu Bakr is flogged whereas anyone who curses 'A'isha is killed. He was asked, "Why is that?" He said, "Whoever attacks her has opposed the Qur'an."

Ibn Sha'ban related this from Malik because Allah has said, **"Allah wishes that you should never repeat the like of it again if you are believers,"** (*Qur'an*: 24.18); so whoever does repeat the like of it has disbelieved.

Qadi 'Iyad also wrote:

There are two positions regarding someone who curses one of the wives of the Prophet ﷺ other than 'A'isha. One position is that he is killed because he has cursed the Prophet ﷺ by cursing his wife. The other is that she is considered to be like the other Companions. He is flogged with the *hadd* for slander. Ibn Sha'ban takes the first position.

Abu Mus'ab related from Malik that someone who curses someone who is connected to the House of the Prophet is given a painful beating and imprisoned for a long time until his repentance is clear because he has made light of what is due to the Messenger ﷺ.

And may the blessings and peace of Allah be on the Prophet Muhammad, and on his Family, and on his Companions, and on all who follow him and them in what they are able with sincerity until the Last Day.

Amin.

The Life of
Muḥammad

صلى الله عليه وسلم

his life based on the earliest sources

Tahia Al-Ismail